Spiders of
the Carolinas

T0151323

Spiders
of the Carolinas

By L.L. Gaddy

Kollath+Stensaas
PUBLISHING

Kollath+Stensaas Publishing
394 Lake Avenue South, Suite 406
Duluth, MN 55802
Office: 218.727.1731
Orders: 800.678.7006
info@kollathstensaas.com
www.kollathstensaas.com

SPIDERS *of the* CAROLINAS

Printed in Korea by Doosan Corporation
10 9 8 7 6 5 4 3 2 1   First Edition

Editorial Director: Mark Sparky Stensaas
Graphic Designer: Rick Kollath

Illustrations by Rick Kollath

ISBN 13: 978-0-9792006-3-2

Table of Contents

Acknowledgements

My father, L. L. Gaddy, Sr., who loved the black water of the Little Pee Dee River in eastern South Carolina, made me appreciate the outdoors and unknowingly got me started on the road to becoming a naturalist. Wandering through the Mountains and Coastal Plain of South Carolina in the 1970s with Rudy Mancke and Edmund Taylor kindled my interest in natural history, especially the diversity and beauty of spiders. Dr. John Morse of Clemson University encouraged and assisted me in putting together the first spider publication in South Carolina—*Common Spiders of South Carolina with an annotated checklist*—in 1985.

On the North Carolina side of the border, I would like to acknowledge the groundwork laid by Dr. Frederick Coyle of Western Carolina University, Cullowhee, North Carolina in arachnological studies. Without Dr. Coyle, our knowledge of North Carolina spiders would be much poorer. He has published many excellent papers on the spiders of North Carolina and has produced numerous graduate students (including naturalists like Bob Dellinger who are equally at ease with plants as well as spiders) who study spiders in North Carolina and other states. His ongoing *Spiders of the Great Smoky Mountain National Park* serves as a basic reference and checklist for any work on North Carolina spiders and is cited repeatedly in this work. Because of Dr. Coyle's fieldwork, the spruce-fir moss spider [*Microhexura montivaga* (Dipluridae)] of the high elevations of North Carolina and Tennessee is one of the few invertebrates listed as "endangered" by the U. S. Fish and Wildlife Service.

Finally, as luck would have it, Sparky Stensaas of Kollath-Stensaas Publishing and I happened to connect at just the right time. With his encouragement and criticism, this little book gradually became what is today.

L. L. "Chick" Gaddy
January 19, 2009

Spiders and Man

He sweeps no cobwebs here, but sells 'em for cut fingers.
—Ben Jonson, *The Staple of News*

Many people fear spiders to the point of arachnophobia. Spiders are fierce predators and do have venom, but deaths from spider bites are extremely rare. One's chances of dying from a lightning strike are much greater than death from a spider bite.

In history, myth, and literature, spiders have assisted man. There is a Hebrew story in which a spider weaves a web, conceals the entrance to a cave and saves David. And, interestingly, there is a similar story about Mohammed's escape from the Coreishites after he had fled Mecca. Byron's "Prisoner of Chillon" said of spiders:

> *With spiders I had friendship made*
> *And watched them in their sullen trade.*

Whitman wrote with wonder of the "noiseless patient spider," and The Count of Monte Cristo used the spider's patient behavior as inspiration to escape from his prison at Chateau d'If.

Spiders are also of medicinal value to man. The ancients used spider webs to stop bleeding and heel cuts and wounds. And in more recent times, some societies thought that swallowing spiders would calm a fever. Up until the mid-1800s, the web of the Medicine Spider, *Coras medicinalis* (Family Amaurobiidae), was prescribed as a narcotic for severe pain. Today, research is being conducted on using spider webs for ligament repair, in scientific instruments, and in textiles. Furthermore, there is some evidence that spider webs may have antibiotic properties.

What are Spiders?

The spider taketh hold with her hands, and is in kings' palaces.
—*Proverbs 30:28.*

L ike insects, spiders are arthropods. They belong to the Phylum *Arthropoda*, the largest phylum in the animal kingdom (remember: Kingdom, Phylum, Class, Order, Family, Genus, Species— *King Phillip Called On Four Gallant Soldiers*, or something like that). Spiders are in the subphylum (of the *Arthropoda*)

This orb-weaving *Argiope* represents what we consider the typical, or "normal", spider.

Not a spider: velvet mite

Chelicerata along with mites, ticks, daddy long-legs, scorpions, and horseshoe crabs. Insects and crustaceans are included in subphylum *Mandibulata*, which have mandibles for biting and crushing, while the *chelicerates* have fangs and poison glands for killing prey and external mouthparts for handling the prey as they ingest it.

Spiders are usually not confused with crustaceans, but they are often thought of as "bugs," along with most insects. Spiders and insects can easily be compared and contrasted. Spiders have eight legs; insects have six. Spiders do not have antennae; insects usually have them. And, finally, spiders have two

Not a spider: tick

body parts; insects have three. Spiders are in the Class *Arachnida*; insects are in the Class *Insecta*. True spiders are arachnids of the Order *Araneae*, or araneids. More about taxonomy in a bit.

Arthropod Summary

	Legs	Body Parts	Antennae	Wings	Gills/Trachea
Arachnids	8	2	0	0	Trachea
Insects	6	3	1 Pair	2 Pair	Gills/Trachea
Crustaceans	10 or more	2	2 Pair	0	Gills
Centipedes	Many *(1 pr./segment)*	1	1 Pair	0	Trachea
Millipedes	Many *(2 pr./segment)*	1	1 Pair	0	Trachea

This chart of Arthropods is a concise way of comparing the different groups. Take a look at how spiders differ from insects, a group with which they are often confused.

A Brief Tour of the Spider

Spiders have eight legs and two body parts; the **cephalothorax** (head and thorax) and the **abdomen**. Interestingly, all eight legs are attached to the cephalothorax, which also contains the mouthparts, eyes, venom glands, brain and the sucking or pre-stomach. The abdomen harbors the heart, intestines, lungs, genitalia and that which makes spiders different from most invertebrates—the silk glands and spinnerets.

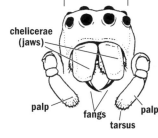

On the front (anterior) portion of the cephalothorax, there are the eye region and the mouth region. Most spiders have eight eyes, although several families only have six eyes. The arrangement and size of the eyes vary considerably from family to family and are often

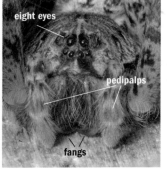

used as distinctive taxonomic features. Some spiders have small eyes and poor eyesight (orb-weavers and web-weavers in general), while other spiders (generally hunting spiders) have excellent eyesight (jumping spiders and wolf spiders).

Below the eyes, there is the mouth surrounded by the **chelicerae**. The chelicerae may have teeth and are tipped

Viewed from above (dorsum)

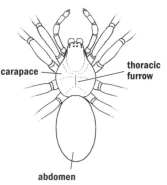

Viewed from below (venter)

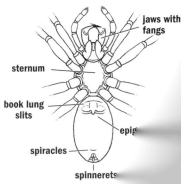

with fangs. They are used to handle prey and to inject poison into the prey. On each side of the chelicerae are **palps** (palpus or palpi), or short, modified legs.

On the tip (**tarsus**) of the palp of male spiders, a boxing glove-like structure is present. This structure serves as a copulatory bulb with the power of suction and

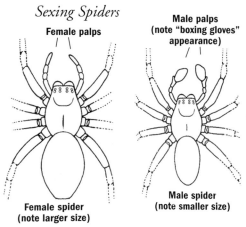

Sexing Spiders

Female palps

Female spider (note larger size)

Male palps (note "boxing gloves" appearance)

Male spider (note smaller size)

ejection of sperm. The sperm is actually produced in the epigastric region of the ventral portion (underside) of the abdomen. The male spins a small "sperm web," ejaculates the sperm onto the web and then sucks it into the bulb on its palp. He keeps it there until he encounters a receptive female. He then inserts the bulb (in a lock-and-key manner) into the female's **epigynum**, also located in the epigastric region of the

The common grass spider —
note the prominent spinnerets.

abdomen. Once inserted, he ejects the sperm from the bulb and the female is inseminated. Spider sex is, therefore, indirect sex; the male and female genitalia never touch.

In addition to the epigynum and the genitalia of the male, the abdomen houses the lungs (several slits on the lower portion), much of the digestive system, the anus, and most importantly, the **spinnerets**. The spin-

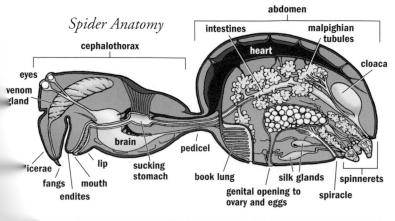

Spider Anatomy

abdomen

cephalothorax

intestines

heart

malpighian tubules

eyes

cloaca

venom gland

brain

pedicel

icerae

lip

sucking stomach

book lung

silk glands

spinnerets

fangs

mouth

genital opening to ovary and eggs

spiracle

endites

nerets are what make a spider a spider. There are two to four pairs (usually three) of spinnerets. They are cylindrical to conical in shape and have several spigots from which many types of silk are produced. Spiders of some families have a sieve-like plate in front of the fourth pair of spinnerets called the **cribellum**. The silk that is pulled through this plate and "teased" is referred to as hackled mesh silk.

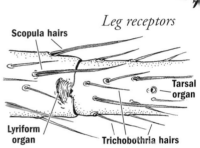

Leg Terminology

coxa (attachment to spider body)

trocanter

femur

patella

tibia

metatarsus

tarsus

Finally, there are the eight legs. The legs of spiders have six sections (**tarsus**, **metatarsus**, **tibia**, **patella**, **femur**, and **trochanter**) and a special section for attachment to the body (**coxa**). Some spiders have smooth legs, while the legs of other spiders have spiny hairs. Some spiders have combs, claws, or teeth on the tarsus, while cribellate spiders have a thick line of hairs or **calamistrum** on the metatarsus.

Leg receptors

Scopula hairs

Tarsal organ

Lyriform organ

Trichobothria hairs

A close-up view of a section of a spider's leg showing four kinds of receptors:

Scopula: simple tactile hairs

Trichobothria: hairs that react to air movement and low-frequency vibrations

Tarsal organs: pores that sense humidity or chemicals

Lyriform organ: a scaly patch that senses leg stress

Venom and Silk

The spider's touch, how exquisitely fine!
Feels at each thread, and lives along the line.
—Alexander Pope, *Essay on Man*

Spiders are well-known for their use of venom to paralyze prey and their prolific production of silk, which is used for wrapping prey, making webs, making egg sacs, and constructing retreats and hibernacula. Other animals used venom for defense, and many insects can make silk, but only spiders employ both venom and silk in their day to day existence.

A *Tetragnatha* spider in the midst of spinning an orb web.

Spiders kill their prey by capturing it and injecting it with venom through the fangs. The venom is usually located in poison glands in the anterior portion of the cephalothorax in most spider families. In the primitive mygalomorphs, the poison glands are found in the basal portion of the chelicerae. One North American family—the *Uloboridae*—does not have poison glands at all. Because of the size of the poison glands, spiders cannot swallow their food. Instead, they eject digestive juices onto the prey to dissolve it. After the prey is in a liquid or near-liquid state, the spiders then ingest it.

It is often said that there are poisonous and non-poisonous spiders. With the exception of the uloborid spiders (see above), all spiders have

The reputation of *Latrodectus* spiders, the infamous black widows, is based on its formidable bite and loveless mating habits.

poison glands. Some spiders, however, have more toxic venom than do others. The poison of two Carolina spiders, the Southern Black Widow (*Latrodectus mactans*) and the Brown Recluse (*Loxosceles reclusa*), is extremely toxic to humans and has, in rare cases, caused death in humans. The Southern Black Widow is native to the entire state and has a neurotoxic venom that attacks the entire body. The poison of the Brown Recluse, on the other hand, is dangerous, but has only local necrotic effects. Furthermore, the Brown Recluse is not native to the Carolinas and has only a spotty distribution in the state. Both spiders are secretive and do not attack humans. The likelihood of being bitten by one

The buffet is ready! A shoreline web is loaded with many victims.

of these spiders is very remote; many more deaths are caused by bee and wasp stings.

If poison makes the spider appear as a beast, then silk reveals the gentler side of spiders. On a dewy Carolina autumn morning, thousands of spectacular dew-dropped Bowl-and-Doily Spider (*Frontinella pyramitela*) webs hang from the tops of low shrubs and tall grasses. In September, every night on your back porch Hentz Orbweavers (*Neoscona crucifera*) weaves her delicate orb to catch the bugs flying into the porch light. And to those impressed by engineering skills, the webs of the Labyrinth Orbweaver (*Metepeira labyrinthea*) and the Basilica Orbweaver (*Mecynogea lemniscata*) are the pinnacle of spider architecture. Spiders, in fact, are classified by their unique web designs.

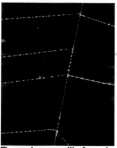
The spokes or radii of a web are non-sticky; allowing the spider to move around freely. But note the tiny packets of "glue" on the spiral.

There are the orbweavers, the cobweb weavers, the sheetweb weavers, the purseweb weavers, and so on.

Silk is made in silk glands at the base of the spider's abdomen. Here, the silk is drawn out through the spinnerets. Different glands make different types of silk. The orbweavers, for example, have seven different types of glands. One gland makes web silk, one gland makes silk for wrapping prey, one gland makes the silk used in egg sac construction, another gland produces draglines and ballooning silk, etc.

Web Types & Construction
By Larry Weber

Virtually every spider uses silk in some capacity, but only the sedentary web hunters use it for snaring prey. Hunting webs are also known as hunting snares. Though sometimes a bit hard to define, web types are usually put into four categories.

1. IRREGULAR COBWEBS. A maze of threads randomly crisscrossing in no particular order. We usually notice cobwebs indoors or near buildings even though they are abundant in the natural landscape as well. In the

A frost-coated cobweb made by a member of the Theridiidae.

Carolinas, it is the members of the family Theridiidae (cobweb weavers), Pholcidae (cellar spiders), and Dictynidae (meshweb weavers) that make irregular cobwebs. Only the outer threads may be sticky, and then only on some webs. Spiders usually sit inverted in the center.

2. SHEET WEBS. Threads anchor a platform or horizontal sheet in grass and bushes. The sheet may be flat, convex or concave. Webs can be complex and beautiful when coated with dew. The well-known Bowl-and-Doily Weaver webs and Filmy Dome Spider (*Neriene radiata*) webs are elaborate examples of sheet webs. Most of the web is non-sticky and only tacky along the trapping threads above the sheet. The best known sheet web family in the Carolinas is the Linyphiidae (sheetweb weavers), but variations of the sheet web

"Bowl-and-doily" sheet web.

or similar ones can also be seen in the Micryphantinae (dwarf spiders) and Hahniidae (hahnid spiders). Spiders often sit inverted beneath the sheet; pulling victims through the bottom of the flat web.

3. FUNNEL WEBS. Sometimes considered to be a variation of the sheet web, funnel webs tend to be flatter and with a funnel-shaped opening in the center. Here the spider sits in retreat, waiting to dash quickly out and grasp tangled prey. The web threads are not sticky. The best known spiders to make this type of web are members of the family Agelenidae (funnel weavers). We often see these webs indoors on windowsills, corners, basements, under eaves and on outbuildings.

Funnel web of a grass spider; family Agelenidae.

4. ORB WEBS. These are the familiar circular webs of the stereotypical spider. Even though several families in our region make these webs; Uloboridae (hackled orbweavers), Tetragnathidae (longjawed orbweavers) and Araneidae (orbweavers), it is this last family that is most commonly observed. Webs are usually vertical and many are high enough above the ground to be called aerial webs. Threads that anchor and extend to the center hub are called spokes (or radii) and are not sticky. Those connecting the spokes and spiraling to the hub are sticky. It is these viscid spirals that hold the prey. The web makers sit in the hub or off to the side. Some will even roll up a nearby leaf and use it as a retreat. Here they wait to feel the vibrations of prey caught in the snare. Eyesight of these orbweavers is so

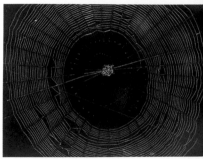

The stereotypical spiderweb; the orb web.

poor that most probably cannot see across their own web, and must rely on feeling alone to locate their catch. Orb webs are abundant in late summer. They may be large and beautiful, but the spider still needs to take them down and remake them each night, or at least every few days. Strangely, spiders of the family Uloboridae make orb webs with no sticky threads.

At sunset, this longjawed orbweaver (*Tetragnathidae*) weaves its hunting snare in a marsh bordering a lake. The web should be loaded with flying insects by morning.

Construction of the orb web always follows the same procedure (see illustration below). First a **bridge** is made. The spider shoots out a thread of sticky silk from its spinnerets. If it catches and the spider feels it catch, a bridge has been established. Next the spider reinforces it by walking back and forth on it, laying down more silk. A thread is fastened in the center of the

Orb web construction

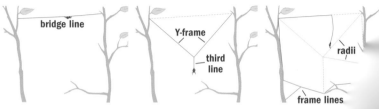

bridge line

Y-frame

third line

radii

frame lines

1. Spider "balloons" out silk. When silk gets snagged, spider tests the hold and then reinforces it with more lines.

2. Spider trails a loose second line, fixed at either end of the bridge line. A third line is made in the middle.

3. Spider returns and spins outer threads and m● (spokes).

last loose horizontal thread and the spider lowers itself down to attach this thread below. Tightening this vertical thread, the spider forms a **hub**. Climbing back up to the hub, and then to the sides, the spider forms a number of **radii** or **spokes**. Spokes are at intervals that allow the spider to step from one to another. Small spiders tend to make webs with more spokes than larger spiders. Next a temporary spiral is made near the hub. Once completed, this is later taken up when the new, sticky and more numerous **spiral** threads are put in place. Sometimes the entire spiral is made up of a single thread; from the outer edge all the way to the center. Between the hub and spirals there is often a space with no spirals. This **free zone** may allow the spider to step between the spokes and switch sides on this vertical web.

Construction of the entire web may take about one-half hour. About five minutes is needed to build the framework and radii. The sticky spiral section requires about twenty minutes.

Some spiders produce a zigzag formation in the hub called a **stabilimentum**. It is most common in the genus *Argiope*. The purpose of this structure has been a mystery, but recent research has shed some possible light on the topic. These special threads stand out in ultraviolet (UV) light possibly attracting insects who can see in UV light. It also may help to disguise the spider who sits right in the middle of the stabilimentum.

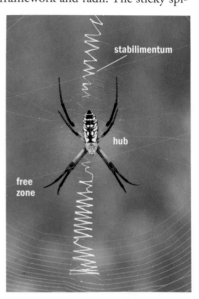

stabilimentum

hub

free zone

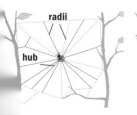

...e the frame and
...e completed, a
...piral hub is spun.

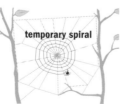

temporary spiral

5. Next, a temporary spiral stabilizes the web and creates "stepping stones" for spinning the sticky snare.

sticky threads in red

6. The spider now retraces its steps, eating the temporary threads, and replacing them with sticky threads.

...er Biology 101

By Larry Weber

Eggs, Egg Sacs & Nursery Webs

Spiders produce eggs during the summer and females deposit these when they are fertilized, about one week after copulation. The number of eggs varies widely; a few species may produce only one or two eggs, some have 25 to 30, many form 100 to 300, and in one situation, more than 2500 eggs were counted in a single egg sac of an orb weaver. Most are about one millimeter in diameter. Groups of these tiny white balls are wrapped in silk by the female to form an egg sac (sometimes called a cocoon). Most sacs are spherical (though some may be other shapes) and five to ten millimeters in diameter.

Many spiders attach this egg sac to the web, usually along the edge. A good example of this can be seen in the Theridiidae (cobweb weavers). Others hide the sac under bark, in a folded leaf or in another convenient hiding place. In many species the female will stand guard over the egg sac. Some species make more than one egg sac and occasionally three or four may be seen in one web at the same time.

Spiders that typically construct silken retreats for their own hiding places will use these same sites to hide the egg sac. Standing guard over these sacs is such a full time commitment for some spiders, that they remain on duty until death.

Four families of spiders are noteworthy when it comes to the handling of their egg sacs. The Pholcidae (cellar spiders) wrap the eggs in just a few thin threads. The actual eggs can be seen right through the scanty covering and it seems the mass will fall apart any second. Once formed, the egg sac is held in the female's jaws as she sits inverted in her irregular cobweb.

A Nursery Web Spider carrying her egg sac before placing it in the specially made nursery web. It is attached to both the spinnerets and her jaws.

The Scytodidae (spitting spiders) carry their eggs too. The egg sac is held in the jaws of the female. She has no web to call home and so carries the sac with her wherever she goes.

Two genera of the Pisauridae (fishing spiders) take this same style of egg-carrying and add a touch of their own. Egg sacs are held by the chelicerae (jaws) but with some threads from the spinnerets also attached. The sac is held more directly under the b... than as in the cellar spiders or spitting s... ders. Seemingly awkward, these spiders age to move about with the huge sac held under their body. No wonder most stay in hiding or limit their movement during this time. Egg-carrying appears to be most inconvenient for the fishing spiders (*Dolomedes*) since they are used to moving about on the surface of the water. Shoreline rock crevices provide safe retreats for females during this stage. A nursery-web spider (*Pisaurina*) female will hold the egg sac in her jaws and spinnerets for a while but then place the sac on a plant leaf, such as a milkweed. She then binds the leaf around her eggs with silk forming an elaborate network of threads and creating a safe hiding place for the young called a nursery web. But just to be sure, the female will stand guard. Usually these large brown-black spiders are seen waiting dutifully, face-down on the stem of the same plant that holds their egg sac.

A female Goldenrod Crab Spider attaches her egg sac to a folded leaf.

Spiderlings

Lycosidae (wolf spiders) are maybe the best known of any spiders when it comes to parental care. The female produces a large egg sac, usually just a bit smaller than the abdomen, and attaches her treasure to the spinnerets. She goes about her business for a couple weeks, wandering around with this white or brown bag on her tail end. (Overwintering adults can be seen with the sac already formed during May, but wolf spiders also produce egg sacs though most

Wolf spiders carry their egg sacs attached to the spinnerets.

of the summer.) Her dedication as a mother does not end with the eggs, though, as she continues to provide transportation after they hatch. The young climb up on her abdomen and stay there for another week to ten days. She does not feed them. They live off their tiny yolk sacs. Since mother wolf spider often stays in hiding while she carries her family, we seldom see this fascinating spectacle of summer.

The tiny baby spiders, known as spiderlings, all hatch from the egg at the same time. Tiny and blind at first, they remain near the egg for a few days. Soon they molt through more advanced stages until begin to resemble the adult spider in body shape and markings. their eyes grow and they develop the ability to spin silk. Unable first, they subsist on an internal yolk sac.

Mama wolf spider pulls baby sitting duty as she carries around all her spiderlings. They cling to specially modified hairs on her back.

Following the next molt, their fangs develop and they are now able to feed. They quickly learn that their own siblings make a tasty and convenient meal, so cannibalism becomes common. To cope with this new threat, the spiderlings start to move away from the family group and disperse. It is also at this time, especially among some of the Theridiidae (cobweb weavers), that a limited social behavior temporarily exists. Not only are the young allowed to stay on the web with the adults, but the females will regurgitate a liquid for the spiderlings to feed on. Of course, young wolf spiders tolerate each other as they ride around on mother's abdomen. True adult social spiders exist only in the tropics.

Most spiderlings are quick to move out on their own. Some of the web spinners form tiny hunting snares for the first time. Others begin hunting in the style of their species while still very small.

Spiderlings (and some adults) engage in a unique form of dispersal known as ballooning. Climbing up fence posts, branches or even blades of grass, they release silk from spinnerets. As the threads lengthen, the wind (even a slight breeze) catches the silk and lifts the little spider into the air as it floats, or "balloons" off to a new site. Though ballooning can carry the small spiders long distances, the average flight may be only inches or a foot; usually to the next branch. Imagine fly-

Ballooning begins with the spiderling raising its abdo and shooting out silk thr When a breeze catches silk, they let go of thei substrate and float aw Most flights are shor few feet.

ing a kite in a wind and letting a strong gust carry you away to a new home. Since many spiders, both young and old, disperse in the fall, ballooning is often associated with autumn. It can, however, take place any time from early spring to well after the leaf drop in late fall/winter. Indeed, with no leaves on the trees and the sun at a low angle, the clear days of late fall are perfect for spotting the abandoned ballooning threads.

The spiderlings continue to grow through the next few weeks and in the style of all arthropods, they molt often. The old skin is shed, leaving behind an empty husk called exuviae. A typical spider molts from four to twelve times before it becomes an adult. The last stage before becoming an adult is called the penultimate stage (or just penultimate). Some spiders may not reach adulthood before late autumn and may win-

Dozens of spiderlings inhabit the web of their mother until sibling-cannibalism makes it an inhospitable place to stay. Dispersal is the next step in life.

ter as a penultimate, maturing in the spring. The stages of growth, those times between molts, are often called instars. For example the fourth

The empty skin (called exuviae) of an immature spider is all that is left following a molt. True spiders do not molt as adults.

instar would be the growth stage between the fourth and fifth molts. With each molt leading to adulthood, missing appendages, usually legs, can be regrown. However, once an adult, a spider is not capable of regenerating new appendages.

After completing the final molt from penultimate to adult, the spiders now have all the needed body parts to mate and reproduce. Also as an adult, they will not molt again. One of the differences between tarantulas (mygalomorphs) and the true spiders (araneomorphs) is that tarantulas molt as adults; true spiders do not.

ourtship & Mating

ders exhibit strange behavior in a number of their life functions, but ng the strangest are courtship and mating. Some males present an t to the female as foreplay. Some males may even guarantee success apping an immature female in silk until she reaches maturity and ates with her. Some of these unusual antics are due to the spider's anatomy. In the male, semen is produced in the testes that are located on the underside of the abdomen. When reaching adulthood and ready to mate, he builds a small "sperm web" where semen is placed. Here he inserts each palp bulb and fills up with semen. Remember, the palp (or pedipalp) is located near the male's face, looking almost like another short pair of legs. He is now ready to search for a receptive female. For mating to be complete, his palp needs to be inserted into her genital opening located near the epigynum on her undersides. To reach this

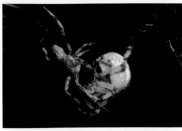

area, the male usually needs to lay across her back (away from her jaws) and reach underneath her abdomen. To get this close, the normally much smaller male needs to court the female to let her know of his intent (see photo on next page).

The smaller male *Araneus* orbweaver (left) approaches the larger female on her web with a series of vibrations and sequential movements that lets her know that he is not prey, but a suitor. He then must reach under her abdomen and inseminate her with the semen stored in his palp bulbs. The whole process is over in seconds.

Courtship varies depending on if the spider is a sedentary web-builder or an active-hunter. With the web-builders, eyesight is usually poor and it is easy for the bigger females to mistake the male for a meal. Because of this, he must approach on her web with a series of vibrations and movements in a sequence that lets her know that he is not prey, but a suitor. When close enough, he rapidly moves in for an instantaneous copulation and sperm transfer. With two palps full of semen, he performs this action twice in quick succession.

Eyesight is considerably better among the wandering spiders, and so courtship is a more visual affair. Here the males may dance before the female, wave the palps or legs (or both) and take on strange poses. Jumping spider males often have striking color patterns on their face and front legs. He performs little dance for the female; raising and waving his front legs, palps or chelicerae while prancing back and forth. He carries on until the female notices and accepts him.

Fishing spiders (*Dolomedes*) also have a unique courtship. The male will vibrate his abdomen on the water's surface in a regular rhythm. The female will sense the even ripples on the water, knowing it is a male and not a struggling insect. Once they get together, a long period of leg-play takes place before they mate.

The tiny male Goldenrod Crab Spider (*Misumena vatia*) cautiously approaches the much larger female. Courtship has begun.

Longjawed orbweavers (*Tetragnatha*) approach each other in the web with jaws agape. The male has special spurs on his jaw which lock her jaws open. Now that she is immobilized he can inseminate her at will. But unfortunately, getting away after mating is not so easy, and some males are captured and eaten.

It is a popular misconception that the male is always killed and eaten by the female (The *Tetragnatha* example above is one of the rare exceptions). Mostly the sexes separate peaceably and the male may mate again. Indeed, sometimes they will share the same web or retreat for a while. Normally, however, the smaller male will die quickly after mating.

Hunting

All spiders are predators and must hunt for their food. Most spiders can be divided into two groups: the web hunters and the active hunters.

When prey hits the web, the spider feels vibrations as the critter struggles to get free. Many moths, dragonflies and grasshoppers are strong enough to be able to escape the web. Typically, those not able to get away from the snare thrash about and get further entangled, struggling until they tire. The spider then moves in with an injection of venom that serves to subdue the prey and liquify its insides. If the spider is hungry, the food is devoured immediately; otherwise, the catch is wrapped in silk for a later meal.

Spiders that do not make webs get their prey in different ways. Some like the crab spiders (thomisids) ambush prey by sitting still and using their camouflaged coloration. Others use good eyesight and quickness to pursue and capture prey. Such active hunters include the jumping spiders (salticids), wolf spiders (lycosids), fishing spiders (pisaurids), ground spiders (gnaphosids) and running crab spiders (philodromids). [They] use fangs and venom to subdue the prey and, just like the web-[build]ers, they use enzymes to partially digest the victim's insides. Larger [spide]rs proceed to crush the insect's exoskeleton as it is sucked dry.

Biogeography
Distribution, Ecology & Evolution

Because spiderlings "balloon" from place to place on light silk lines (the "gossamer" we see in autumn), spiders are widely distributed. Few endemic species are found, except on islands and in caves. Many species found in the Carolinas are found throughout North America, or, at least, eastern North America. And some species are cosmopolitan or cosmotropical, being found around the world.

Because spiders are predatorial, they are food generalists and do not have to live near one food plant or in one habitat. Most species, therefore, range between several habitats and are usually not confined to one habitat or microhabitat. There are, of course, exceptions. Some spiders are found only in houses and buildings; some species prefer forests; and some are found primarily near water.

The many species and families of spiders attest to a range a fascinating evolutionary divergence. The orb web, for example, has evolved twice in spiders—once in the Araneidae family (orbweavers) and once in the Uloboridae family (hackled orbweavers), two families that are not otherwise closely related. Some crab spiders (Thomisidae) have mastered the art of near perfect camouflage and even change colors when they move from flower to flower. Spider mimicry is just being studied and understood. Most predators avoid eating ants (or anything that resembles the ant form) because ants are are infused with formic acid. Because of this, some hunting spiders have evolved bodily shapes that are amazingly similar to some species of ants and have adapted a slow, deliberate ant-like mode of locomotion. Recently, many spider antmimics have been grouped in a new family, the Corinnidae. But ant-mimics also are found in the Clubionidae, Gnaphosidae and Salticidae families. In the salticid (jumping) spiders, *Sarinda hentzii* mimics red *Formica* ants, *Synemosyna formica* mimics carpenter ants and *Peckhamia* ants resemble reddish-black ants of the genus *Crematogaster*. Some spiders even mimic female velvet ants, which are really mutillid wasps mimicking ants.

Physiographic Provinces

Bioregions of the Carolinas

There are three major physiographic provinces in the Carolinas: the Blue Ridge, the Piedmont and the Coastal Plain. The Piedmont is often broken down into the Outer and Inner (or Upper and Lower) Piedmont, and the Coastal Plain is frequently divided into three sub-provinces—the Sandhills, the Inner Coastal Plain and the Outer Coastal Plain. The Outer Coastal Plain can also be divided into the Northern and Southern Coastal Plains.

The Blue Ridge Province, often called the "Mountain" Province, is found in the western part of the Carolinas. Here, elevations begin at just over 1000 feet and extend up to 6,684 feet. The geology here is a mixture of granitic and meta-morphic formations, and the vegetation is dominat-ed by mixed hardwood forests. The

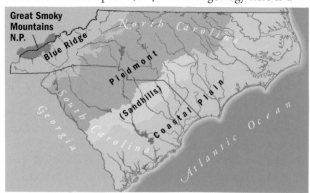

Blue Ridge spider fauna has more northern elements than does the spider fauna of the rest of the state.

The Piedmont consists of rolling hills, occasional monadnocks, and deep valleys and ravines. It extends from the Blue Ridge province to the Fall Line (the line separating the Piedmont and Coastal Plain). The geology of the Piedmont is complex with metamorphic belts, granitic plutons, and diabase dikes. Elevations range from just over 1000 feet to around 100 feet near the Fall Line. The spider fauna here is more closely related to the Blue Ridge fauna than to the Coastal Plain fauna; however-er, there are numerous disjunct distributions where Coastal Plain spiders are found in the Piedmont.

The Coastal Plain is a sedimentary plain that extends from the Fall Line near Columbia and Raleigh to the Atlantic Coast. Here, metamor-phic and igneous rocks are absent and elevations are generally less than 100 feet. Noteworthy geological features of the Coastal Plain—both with spider subfaunas of their own—are the Sandhills, a well-defined belt of coarse-sand hills in the Inner Coastal Plain, and the barrier islands, a line of subtropical islands just off the coast.

Taxonomy 101

In the taxonomic scheme of things, the Garden Spider (*Argiope aurantia*) is:

KINGDOM – Animalia

PHYLUM – Arthropoda

SUBPHYLUM – Chelicerata

CLASS – Arachnida

ORDER – Araneae

FAMILY – Araneidae

GENUS – Argiope

SPECIES – aurantia

There are two large Suborders of the Order *Araneae*:

Orthognatha (mygalomorphs): the primitive spiders— the trapdoor spiders, the tarantulas, and the Purseweb spiders;

Mygalomorph chelicerae and fangs move downward.

and:

Labidognatha (araneomorphs): the more advanced or "true" spiders.

Araneomorph chelicerae and fangs move laterally.

Taxonomy

Spiders are classified in groups based on several distinctive taxonomic characters. Families are separated based on the type of chelicerae (mygalomorph or araneomorph), the presence of a sieve-plate or cribellum (cribellate and ecribellate spiders), or the kind of web or lack of web in the given group of spiders. Spider taxonomists also use the shape of the genitalia to separate different species of spiders in the same genus.

Here, we are more concerned with rapid identification of common species and will concentrate on web type (or lack of web) and spider morphology and color patterns.

Carolina Spiders

The first known publication on South Carolina spiders was Howard's "List of the Invertebrate Fauna of South Carolina" (1881). It listed 251 species of spiders from the state. Chamberlin and Ivie (1944) listed 552 species from the "Georgia" region, an area they defined to include much of South Carolina, all of Georgia and some of northern Florida. Other publications on Carolina spiders include Barnes and Barnes (1955) (spiders of broomsedge fields in the Piedmont of North Carolina), Berry (1970) (North Carolina Piedmont old field spiders), Pendleton (1974) (spiders of Santee Swamp in South Carolina), Kelley (1979) (spiders of a granitic flatrock in the Piedmont of South Carolina), Gaddy (1981) (forest spiders on South Carolina barrier islands), Lee (1981) (spiders in South Carolina peach orchards), Roach and Edwards (1984) (a checklist of the jumping spiders of South Carolina), Gaddy (1987) (orb-weavers in Mountain forests in South Carolina) and Wharton et al. (1981) (a list of spiders of bottomland hardwoods in South Carolina). In 1985 Gaddy and Morse published *Common Spiders of South Carolina with an annotated checklist* (Gaddy and Morse, 1985), which included 326 documented species of spiders for South Carolina with 164 species whose ranges overlap the state but have not be collected in the state. The spider fauna of the Great Smoky Mountains National Park in North Carolina has been and is still being studied by Coyle (2008). To date, he has recorded approximately 500 species from the park, including around 20 species new to science. From the Canadian-zone spruce-fir forests of the high Smokies to the subtropical barrier islands of South Carolina, a broad range of climates and habitats are present in the Carolinas. Based upon that fact and the existing publications on spiders in the Carolinas, it can be estimated that the total spider fauna probably approaches or exceeds 600 species.

The Carolinas have at least ten endemic species of spiders. Six of the endemics are in the genus *Nesticus* [*N. brimleyi*, *N. carolinensis* (the Linville Caverns spider), *N. cooperi*, *N. crosbyi*, *N. nasicus*, *N. silvanus*] (Family Nesticidae), a genus primarily of cave dwellers (see Gertsch, 1984 and Coyle and McGarity, 1991), all rare species only found in North Carolina. Two other North Carolina endemics are lampshade weavers (see pages 28-31)—*Hypochilus sheari* and *Hypochilus coylei*—found in mountain gorges, where they are also rare. The small Tuscarora Orbweaver [*Araneus tuscarora* (Araneidae)] is also a North Carolina endemic, being known only from Durham, Lee and Montgomery Counties (Levi, 1973). In South Carolina, the extremely rare purse-web endemic *Sphodros coylei* (Coyle's purseweb spider) is known only from the Clemson area in Pickens County and nowhere else. Another rare and fairly famous spider, the Spruce-Fir Moss Spider [*Microhexura montivaga* (Dipluridae)] weaves tube webs in moss mats in rocky, high-elevation spruce (*Picea*)-fir (*Abies*) forests in North Carolina and Tennessee. This spider, which is federally-listed as endangered by the U.S. Fish and Wildlife Service, is known from seven mountain tops (including Mount LeConte, Grandfather Mountain and Mount Mitchell) in eight counties in the two states and is the only Carolina spider of the federal endangered species list.

Unfortunately, little is known of most of the rare species and endemics in the Carolinas. Here, only the most common and well-known spiders of the two states are discussed. Let it be understood, however, that the omission of any species of spider found in the two states does not in any way serve as a comment on their importance in the total fauna of the two states.

How to use this Field Guide

*S*piders of the Carolinas is designed to make field identification easier for you, the reader. Through the use of color photos, arrows pointing to field marks, size scales, gender symbols and habitats, we have made a handy, compact and easy to use guide. It is small enough to tuck into any daypack.

Coverage

We have made no attempt to include all species, or even all the genera, of North and South Carolina's spider fauna. Instead, we have highlighted the most common, several of the bizarre, a few of the most colorful and, yes, also the dangerously poisonous spiders. Gaddy and Morse (1985) listed spiders from 35 families occurring in South Carolina. Herein, spiders from 26 families are treated.

Not all species are found in any single area. Habitat preferences spread species out. The Carolinas are a mosaic of preferred spider habitats; from barrier islands, swamps and rivers to deciduous woods, piedmont, meadows, monadnocks, ravines and suburban yards. And don't forget the inside of your own home; spiders are year-round residents of even the tidiest houses.

Organization

Spiders—order Araneae—are organized by families and then broken down further into genera, and where possible, species. We have arranged the spider families in standard scientific order. Within each family, the genera are simply arranged alphabetically by Latin name. There are a few exceptions where layout dictated a slight reshuffling of the order.

At the start of each family is a page or two highlighting the general characteristics of the members of that family. Illustrations show typical eye pattern (a useful diagnostic tool), general shape, possibly a web and an actual-size silhouette.

The hope is that with experience in the field using this guide, you will gradually learn to identify spiders to family. This is a major step and one that will lessen your frustration and increase your enjoyment in identifying our eight-legged friends.

Spider Names

Like all organisms, spiders are given a scientific name. Unfortunately, many spiders do not have a common name. The common names are the English names most amateur naturalists use, while the scientific or Latin names tend to be the spoken word of entomologists and arachnologists. In this book we list all spiders according to the *Common Names of Arachnid 2003,* a booklet put out by the American Arachnological Society (also at www.americanarachnology.org).

When no common name exists for a species of spider, we have manufactured one from the Latin specific epithet. For example, *Theridion deum*—a species of cobweb weaver that has no official common name—becomes the Leafy Cobweb Weaver as "frondeum" refers to leaves. When the Latin specific epithet has no relevant meaning we simply call the spider by the group name with a "sp." afterwards (short for "species"). If multiple species are being referred to, the abbreviation is "spp."

All common names referring to a specific species will be capitalized. For example, "black widow" is not capitalized because it can refer to several species such as Northern Black Widow, Brown Widow and Southern Black Widow.

The family name is listed at the bottom of all the species account pages.

Black size-bars show average legspan (entire bar length) of males (M) and females (F). Distance to first white bar is body length

Arrows highlight easily recognizable features to aid in identification.

Photos on the right side of the spread highlight sexual dimorphism, webs, hunting techniques and/or unique behaviors.

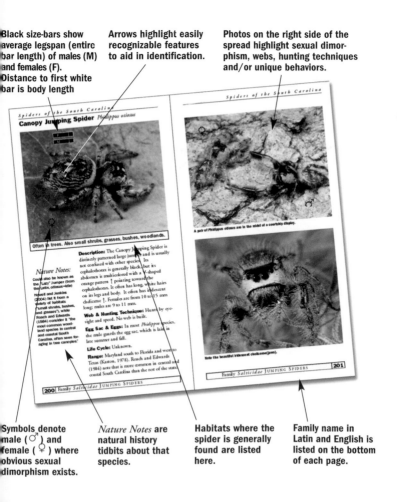

Symbols denote male (♂) and female (♀) where obvious sexual dimorphism exists.

Nature Notes **are natural history tidbits about that species.**

Habitats where the spider is generally found are listed here.

Family name in Latin and English is listed on the bottom of each page.

Purseweb Spiders
Family Atypidae

Description

This family and the following two families represent the Suborder Orthognatha (of order Aranea), often called the Mygalomorphae, or the tarantulas. The poison glands are located in the large chelicerae, which move parallel to the plane of the body.

Similar Spiders

These spiders have stout bodies and legs and are similar in appearance to other mygalomorphs or tarantula-like spiders.

Hunting Techniques/Web

The Atypidae are, as the family name indicates, the "atypical" tarantulas. These spiders make tubular silk webs that extend above ground and are used as retreats and prey-catching devices.

Diversity (Species Richness/Range)

Around five species known from North America. Three species of this family are known from the Carolinas. Coyle (2008) reports *Sphodros niger* from the Smokies.

Purseweb Spiders (Family Atypidae)

Page 23 Common Purseweb Spider (*Sphodros rufipes*)

Typical *Atypide* purseweb spider

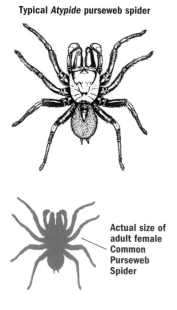

Actual size of adult female Common Purseweb Spider

The "purse web"

Common Purseweb Spider *Sphodros rufipes*

Rich upland woods, barrier islands and large floodplain swamps.

Description: Purseweb spiders can be easily recognized by their large chelicerae ↑ (including fangs), which are nearly as long as the cephalothorax. The abdomen also has long spinnerets ↑. *Sphodros rufipes* has red legs. Females are around 25 mm in length, while males are about 15 mm.

Web & Hunting Technique: Generally lean their tube webs against the base of a tree trunk or a rock. The tube extends from several inches below ground to as much as a foot above.

The female lives in a camouflaged silk-lined tube. When insects walk up the outside of the sticky tube, the female bites through the tube and kills them. Later, she cuts the tube open and pulls them through. Males are wandering hunters and do not make webs.

Life Cycle: Long-lived (1 to 5 years).

Range: Found from New England south to Florida and west to Louisiana.

Nature Notes:

According to Gaddy and Morse (1985), there are two known *Sphodros* species in South Carolina and three additional species whose ranges overlap the state.

This is the "purse web" that gives this spider its common name.

Foldingdoor Spiders
Family Antrodiaetidae

Description
The foldingdoor spiders are mygalomorphs with large chelicerae and short and stout bodies.

Similar Spiders
Similar to spiders of the families Atypidae, Ctenizidae and other mygalomorphs—primitive spiders with horizontally-oriented chelicerae.

Habitat
The foldingdoor spiders burrow into the soils in open areas where bare soil is exposed.

Hunting Techniques/Web
They hunt from the door of a silk-lined burrow, pouncing on prey that walks by the tube's opening.

Diversity (Species Richness/Range)
Thirteen species are known from North America. The one species known from the Carolinas constructs a burrow with a trapdoor that folds in the middle.

Folding Trapdoor Spiders (Family Antrodiaetidae)
Page 25   Foldingdoor Spider (*Antrodeaetus unicolor*)

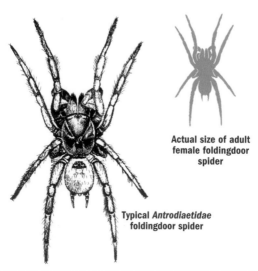

Actual size of adult female foldingdoor spider

Typical *Antrodiaetidae* foldingdoor spider

Foldingdoor Spider *Antrodiaetus unicolor*

F

M

Cliff banks and exposed roadcuts.

Description: The Foldingdoor Spider is brown to reddish-brown. Like other mygalomorphs, it has huge chelicerae ↑ and prominent spinnerets. Females are around 20 mm in length, while males are about 17 mm.

Web & Hunting Technique: The burrow is silk-lined with a trap door that folds as it opens or closes.

The females probably capture most prey by hiding in the burrow and pouncing on passersby. Both the female and the male, however, are known to hunt along the ground a considerable distance from the burrow.

Life Cycle: Unknown; but because it is a mygalomorph, it is probably long-lived.

Range: Appears to be present only in the Mountains and Piedmont of the Carolinas. It ranges from New York south to Georgia and west to Arkansas.

Nature Notes:

Its burrows are difficult to spot because, the door, which often has a fold down the middle, is camouflaged with sticks and/or mosses.

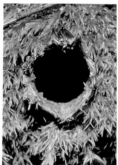

A burrow with the folding door removed.

Trapdoor Spiders
Family Ctenizidae

Description
Large-bodied spiders with large chelicerae and short, stout legs.

Similar Spiders
Similar to spiders of the families Atypidae, Antrodiaetidae and other mygalomorphs—primitive spiders with horizontally-oriented chelicerae.

Habitat
Woodland edges and open areas—generally not species of forests.

Hunting Techniques/Web
The trapdoor spiders build tubular silk-line burrows with a silky trapdoor that may be open and closed by the spider or by a thread attached to the spider's leg.

Observations
Trapdoor spiders are rarely seen outside of their burrows except after periods of flooding or heavy rains. *Myrmeciophila fluviatilis*, rare in South Carolina, is known to eat ants (as its name indicates).

Diversity (Species Richness/Range)
As many as 30 species in North America. In the Carolinas, two species are known.

Trapdoor Spiders (Family Ctenizidae)
Page 27   Southern Trapdoor Spider (*Ummidia audouini*)

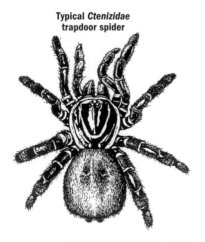

**Typical *Ctenizidae*
trapdoor spider**

**Actual size of adult
trapdoor spider**

Southern Trapdoor Spider *Ummidia audouini*

F
M

Woodlands and woods edges.

Description: Usually completely black. This large spider is wide-bodied and has enormous chelicerae. The legs and the carapace of the cephalothorax are shiny black. Females are 28 mm in length; males to 15 mm long.

Web & Hunting Technique: The female captures prey by hiding in the burrow and pouncing on passers-by. Both the female and the male, however, are known to hunt along the ground a distance from the burrow.

Burrow is silk-lined with a large hinged, camouflaged trap door up to one inch in diameter.

Egg Sac & Eggs: Not seen; however, I once happened up a conglomeration of tens of hatchlings. It was autumn, and they were at the top a small shrub trying to balloon away.

Life Cycle: Unknown; but because it is a mygalomorph, it is probably long-lived.

Range: Ranges from Virginia to Florida and west to Illinois and Oklahoma.

Nature Notes:

Because of its secretive nature, these spiders are usually seen only after heavy rains (when burrows are flooded) or when they are accidentally dug out of the ground.

On my farm in the Sandhills of South Carolina, I had one near my pumphouse. The *Ummidia* would keep his trap door open (I could see his shining eyes in the flashlight beam) until I got about ten feet from the burrow and would then quickly pull the trap-door shut. Because the trap door was so well camouflaged, it took me several attempts to find the burrow in daylight.

Lampshade Weavers
Family Hypochilidae

Description
The lampshade weavers are probably the most primitive of the araneo-morphs (or labidognatha). They have extremely long legs (several times the length of the body) and are usually found in webs. The labium and the sternum are fused, and these spiders have four book lungs.

Similar Spiders
There is some resemblance to the cellar spiders (Pholcidae), but cellar spiders are rarely seen in rocky areas and have a different body structure from the lampshade weavers.

Habitat
Gorges and deep ravines; under rocks and rock overhangs.

Hunting Techniques/Web
The adults live in the top of the lampshade-shaped web, upside down, and hanging from the underside of a rock. They eat prey that is caught in the margins of the lampshade.

Observations
The male, which has longer front legs (Legs I and II) than the female, supposedly steps over the outer portion of the lampshade to get into the female's retreat. These spiders have a two year life cycle from spiderling to adult.

Diversity (Species Richness/Range)
Fewer than ten species known from North America (Forster, Platnick, and Gray, 1987); three species are found in the Carolinas.

Lampshade Weavers (Family Hypochilidae)
Page 30   Pocock Lampshade Weaver (*Hypochilus pocockii*)

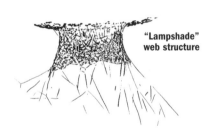

"Lampshade" web structure

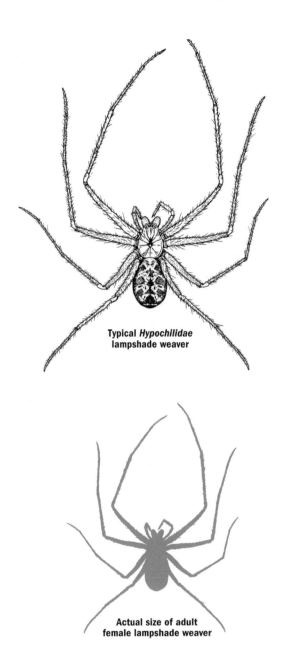

**Typical *Hypochilidae*
lampshade weaver**

**Actual size of adult
female lampshade weaver**

Pocock Lampshade Weaver *Hypochilus pocockii*

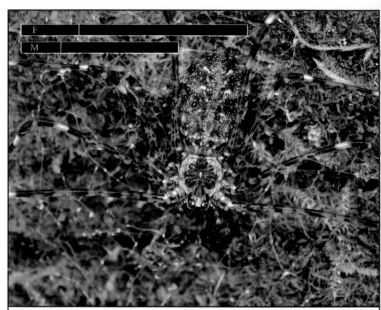

Mountain gorges and deep ravines under overhanging rocks.
The spider usually prefers humid but not wet sites.

Nature Notes:

Formerly known as *Hypochilus thorellii*.

Because the female stays in the center of the lampshade web, she is easily approached. If disturbed, she pushes her body up and down on her long legs, appearing to do bouncy push-ups.

Venom glands in the *Hypochilus* are located in the chelicerae, instead of in the head.

Description: Pocock Lampshade Weaver, like its congeners, is a long-legged grayish spider. The legs resemble those of the cellar spiders (*Pholcus* spp.) in their proportion to the spider's body length. This lampshade weaver holds its long front legs (Leg I) folded while is hangs inside of its lampshade. Females 14 to 16 mm long; males 10 to 11 mm.

Web & Hunting Technique: The web is in the shape of a lampshade with the top of the "shade" flush against the underside of a rock. The spider hangs upside down, legs on the rock, in the middle of the top of the lampshade.

The female rarely leaves the web. The male roams somewhat and is known to climb over the edge of the "lampshade" with his extremely long legs to mate with the female.

The distinctive undersides of the Pocock Lampshade Weaver.

Mate guarding is a mating ritual of the males.

This is the lampshade-shaped web that gives this spider its common name.

Life Cycle: Unlike most spiders, Pocock Lampshade Weaver has a two-year life cycle. Both sexes are immature the first year of their life.

Range: In the Carolinas this spider is found ...ly in the Mountain Province. *Hypochilus ...ockii* also occurs in Virginia, North Carolina, ...rgia and Tennessee.

Crevice Weavers (Hibernating Spiders)
Family Filistatidae

Description
The Filistatidae is a small family of cribellate spiders with a calamistrum. The females are usually black to brown and the males are often brown. The eyes are bunched on a prominent central mound.

Similar Spiders
The males of *Kukulcania hibernalis* have often been mistaken for *Loxosceles* (Brown Recluse) spiders. The Brown Recluse, however, has only six eyes in three pairs. Females of *Kukulcania* look like dark wolf spiders, but the eye pattern and the presence of the cribellum and the calamistrum separates them from lycosids.

Habitat
In buildings and houses.

Hunting Techniques/Web
The female makes a hackled web retreat in window jambs, between boards in barns, between wood shingles on houses and in door jambs. The outer web lines can be felt by the female in the retreat when prey walk or land on the web. The males are often seen running around on the floor of buildings.

face
(jaws obscured
by pedipalps)

Observations
Kukulcania hibernalis appears to hibernate (one of its common names is "Southern Hibernating Spider") and can live for several years.

Diversity (Species Richness/Range)
Less than ten species are known in North America; only one species is known from the Carolinas.

Crevice or Hibernating Spiders (Family Filistatidae)
Page 33 Southern House Spider
(*Kukulcania hibernalis*)

Actual size of
adult female
crevice weaver

Typical
Filistatidae
crevice weaver

Southern House Spider *Kukulcania hibernalis*

| F | |
| M | |

Houses, barns, garages and old buildings.

Description: A large cribellate spider. Female is usually black but male is brown with long front legs and a small violin-shaped marking on the carapace. These two characters have led to the spider being mistaken for a Brown Recluse. Females 13 to 19 mm; males 9 to 10 mm.

Web & Hunting Technique: The female constructs a conspicuous, hackled white web in building crevices. The web is roughly radially symmetrical and has a central opening or hole. The female stays in the back of the web by day and sits near the opening at night.

The male roams and hunts like a wolf spider r fishing spider.

e Cycle: Active year round. Common in ter (on warm days).

ze: Found throughout the Carolinas, but common in the Coastal Plain. Known only he southeastern states west to east Texas.

Nature Notes:

Sometimes called the "Hibernating Spider."

Formerly known as *Filistata hibernalis.*

The female is reclusive and harmless. The male, however, is often found running through houses and appears to be dangerous. I, however, know of no bites from this species.

Almost every old barn seen in the Coastal Plain has several. I once lived on a South Carolina barrier island in an old house. There I had a Southern House Spider in a window jam; the spider lived for three years.

Sixeyed Sicariid Spiders
Family Sicariidae

Description
The Sixeyed Sicariid Spiders were formerly in the family Loxoscelidae and were often referred to as the "Brown" Spiders. This is the family of the Brown Recluse and other recluse spiders. All spiders of the genus have six eyes in three triads and have the outline of a violin on the carapace of the cephalothorax.

Similar Spiders
Males of the Southern House Spider (*Kulkania hibernalis*) are similar in appearance to the Brown Recluse.

Habitat
Generally in and around houses and outbuildings.

Hunting Techniques/Web
The female makes a small web for catching prey; the male is a wandering spider and hunts on the move.

Observations
Nearly all species in this genus have dangerous venom, but *L. reclusa* and *L. laeta* appear to be the most harmful.

Diversity (Species Richness/Range)
There are reportedly five native species of *Loxosceles* in the United States. The introduced *Loxosceles laeta* from South America is common in the Los Angeles area. There is only one species in the Carolinas and it is probably not native to either state.

Sixeyed Sicariid Spiders (Family Sicariidae)
Page 36   Brown Recluse (*Loxosceles reclusa*)

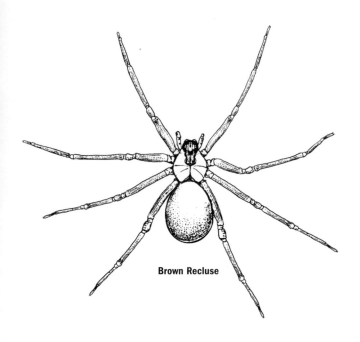

Brown Recluse

face

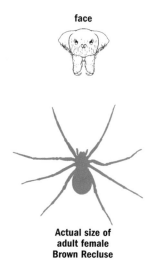

**Actual size of
adult female
Brown Recluse**

Brown Recluse (Violin Spider) *Loxosceles reclusa*

F	
M	

Attics, basements (often among stored newspaper and clothes), barns and outbuildings. Rock piles, bark, under logs.

Nature Notes:

The Brown Recluse, like the Southern Black Widow, is often found in old shoes. When someone puts on one of the old shoes, they are bitten on the toe and may not realize it until much later.

THE BROWN RECLUSE IS VENOMOUS AND IS A DANGEROUS SPIDER; CHECK OLD SHOES OR CLOTHING THAT HAS NOT BEEN WORN IN A LONG TIME BEFORE PUTTING ON.

Description: The Brown Recluse is a six-eyed, mostly brown, spider. The distinctive identifying features of this dangerous spider are: 1) the "violin" (the spider is sometimes called the Violin Spider) on the carapace↑ (dorsum) of the cephalothorax and 2) the extremely long front legs (Leg I and Leg II) of the spider (in the female, Leg I is over four times as long as the cephalothorax). Females have a light brown body with a lighter brown (beige) abdomen; males often have a darker abdomen. In both sexes the violin is dark brown. The males of the Southern House Spider (*Kukulcania hibernalis*) are often thought to be Brown Recluses. Females are around 9-10 mm in length, while males a about 8 mm long.

Web & Hunting Technique: The f makes a small, nondescript web; the hunts for prey.

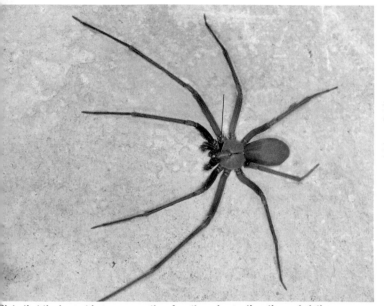

Note that the longest legs are more than four times longer than the cephalothorax.

Life Cycle: Active year round.

Range: Brown Recluses are not found in the wild in the Carolinas. They are generally found in and around dwellings and are believed to have been brought here by humans moving from the mid-South where the spiders are native (Ohio south to Georgia and west to Texas and Nebraska). The spider has been reported from all over the Carolinas, but it does not appear to be abundant in the state.

A close look at the violin marking on the carapace.

Spitting Spiders
Family Scytodidae

Description
Brown and white spiders with distinctively-sloping cephalothorax.

Similar Spiders
None.

Habitat
Houses and outbuildings.

carapace viewed from the side

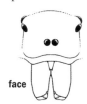

face

Hunting Techniques/Web
These spiders actually spit a sticky substance onto the prey. The prey is temporarily stuck, long enough for the spitting spider to attack. They often make a silk retreat, but no prey-catching web is usually seen.

Observations
The spitting spiders are common household spiders that are known to have very large poisonous glands. Envenomation of humans, however, does not appear to be common.

Diversity (Species Richness/Range)
There are seven species of spitting spiders in the United States. The Common Spitting Spider, which is the only one known in the Carolinas, is thought by some researchers to have been introduced from Europe.

Spitting Spiders (Family Scytodidae)
Page 39   Common Spitting Spider
            (*Scytodes thoracica*)

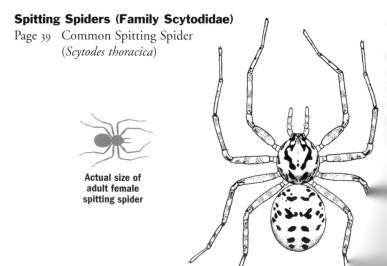

Actual size of adult female spitting spider

Common Spitting Spider *Scytodes thoracica*

F

M

Mainly in buildings; bathrooms, basements, brick walls.

Description: The Common Spitting Spider is a six-eyed spider. The eyes are arranged in pairs in a triangle, giving the spider the appearance of having two large eyes and a "nose." It is yellow with a complex pattern of black markings. The cephalothorax is high and slopes steeply down to the chelicerae ↑. Females are 4 to 5.5 mm in length, while males are 3.5 to 4 mm.

Web & Hunting Technique: Does not make a web; the male and female both hunt. The spider spits a sticky secretion on passing insects. The sticky substance immobilizes the prey long enough for the spider to attack and kill. They have unusually large poison glands.

Egg Sac & Eggs: A conglomeration of small, clear eggs that look like little bubbles ↑. Often carried around in the chelicerae of the female for long periods.

Life Cycle: Active year round.

Range: Found throughout the Carolinas and most of eastern North America.

Nature Notes:

Emerton (1902) thought that this spider was introduced from Europe.

When observed with a hand lens, the spider has a distinctive "face" with two eyes (actual two pair of small eyes), a nose (another pair of eyes) and a beard (the hairs on the chelicerae).

Protective mothers: Females use their chelicerae to carry the distinctive egg sacs for a long while.

Cellar Spiders
Family Pholcidae

Description
The cellar spiders have extremely long legs (several times the length of the body) and are usually found in webs.

Similar Spiders
Brown Recluses and Southern House Spiders look somewhat like cellar spiders, but they have much shorter legs, larger bodies and are generally not found in open webs.

Habitat
Basements and cellars.

Hunting Techniques/Web
Cellar spiders are generally found in large, chaotic webs in the corners of basements or cellars. Here, they hang upside-down and catch prey.

Egg Sacs and Eggs
Eggs sacs are held in the fangs of the female.

Diversity (Species Richness/Range)
Approximately 20 species known from North America; three species are found in the Carolinas (Gaddy and Morse, 1985).

Cellar Spiders (Family Pholcidae)
Page 41   Longbodied Cellar Spider (*Pholcus phalangioides*)

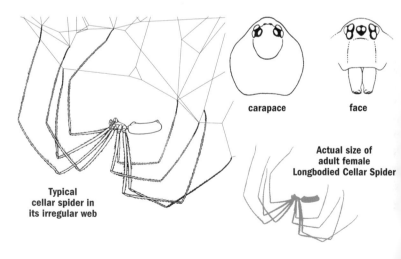

carapace

face

Typical cellar spider in its irregular web

Actual size of adult female Longbodied Cellar Spider

Longbodied Cellar Spider *Pholcus phalangioides*

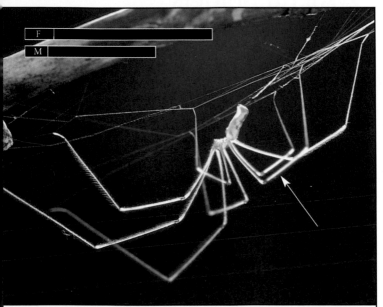

F

M

Found in cellars and basements, especially where insecticides have not been used. In the wild, caves and under rock overhangs.

Description: The Longbodied Cellar Spider is a very distinctive species and cannot be confused with any other spider. The body is a nondescript grey-brown, but its legs are approximately six to eight times longer than the body ↑. The body of the female is 7 to 8 mm in length, while the male's body is 6 mm.

Web & Hunting Technique: The female makes a large irregular web, usually in a dark corner of a basement or cellar. She hangs upside down in the middle of the web with legs partially folded.

Egg Sac & Eggs: The female holds the small egg sac, which is often mistaken for prey, in her jaws.

Life Cycle: Active year round.

Range: This spider is abundant in cellars and basements throughout the Carolinas. Its range encompasses all of the United States.

Nature Notes:

Sometimes the Longbodied Cellar Spiders are mistaken for harvestmen of the Order Opiliones and called "Daddy Longlegs (Granddaddy Longlegs)." Unlike true spiders, the cephalothorax and the abdomen in the *Opiliones* are fused and appear rounded.

Dysderid Spiders
Family Dysderidae

Description
This is a small family of spiders with only one genus. Our species is bright orange-red and has extremely obvious, protruding chelicerae with long fangs. They have six eyes like the segesteriids.

Similar Spiders
No similar spiders or families.

Habitat
Under stones and loose bark.

Hunting Techniques/Web
These spiders construct a silken retreat, but generally hunt outside of the retreat.

Diversity (Species Richness/Range)
Dysdera crocata is a cosmopolitan species, found generally all over the world. There are over 100 other species in the genus *Dysdera* in Europe and the Middle East; only one species is known from the Carolinas (Gaddy and Morse, 1985).

Dysderid Spiders (Family Dysderidae)
Page 43   Orange Spider or Woodlouse Spider (*Dysdera crocata*)

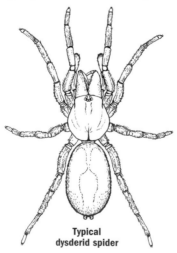

**Typical
dysderid spider**

Orange Spider (Woodlouse Spider) *Dysdera crocata*

F

M

Under stones and debris lying on the ground and under loose tree bark.

Description: This spider is a bright orange to reddish-orange spider. It has six eyes and unusually large chelicerae with long, prominent fangs ↑. The abdomen is often whitish to light brown and not as brightly colored as the remainder of the body. Females are 11 to 15 mm in length; males are 9 to 10 mm long.

Web & Hunting Technique: Hunts by night; remains in a silken retreat by day.

Egg Sac & Eggs: According to Comstock (1940), the female lays eggs in her silken retreat. The spiderlings are thought to remain with the mother until they are large enough to disperse.

Life Cycle: Probably overwinters as an adult. May live several years.

Range: Few records are known from the Carolinas; the spider is probably overlooked. This is a cosmopolitan species, found all over the world.

Nature Notes:

In Europe, this spider is called the "woodlouse" spider, presumably because it eats woodlice ("rolly-polies"), small crustaceans of the Order Isopoda.

In England, Hillyard (1994) points out that its bite has been reported to cause local swelling and dizziness.

Because of this spider's hairless body and long chelicerae (especially long fangs), it is often erroneously thought to be a mygalomorph (tarantula-type) spider.

Hackled Orbweavers
Family Uloboridae

Description

The uloborids are orbweavers that are not araneid (or true) orbweavers. This is what biologists call "convergent evolution." The orb web has evolved twice—in two separate, distantly-related, families. The hackled orbweavers are cribellate spiders. They make horizontal webs and have humps on their abdomens.

Similar Spiders

Webs of the uloborids might be mistaken for those of the Araneidae or Theridiosomatidae, but the spiders can never be confused.

Habitat

Shrubs and low limbs in forests; also disturbed woods around dwellings.

Hunting Techniques/Web

Some species in this family build their webs only at night. Spiders of the genus *Uloborus* build a very symmetrical, horizontally-oriented, orb web with a stabilimentum of hackled silk in the middle of the web.

Diversity (Species Richness/Range)

There are around 15 species of this family in North America. In the Carolinas, three species are known (Gaddy & Morse, 1985).

Hackled Orbweavers (Family Uloboridae)

Page 45   Triangle Weaver (*Hyptiotes cavatus*)
Page 46   Featherlegged Orbweaver (*Uloborus glomosus*)

face

spinnerets (note cribellum ↑)

Featherlegged Orbweaver

Triangle Weaver

Triangle Weaver *Hyptiotes cavatus*

F
M

♀

Dry woods, woodland edges, floodplains, swamps and around dwellings.

Description: The Triangle Weaver is also a cribellate spider. The general color of this spider is brown to gray. The abdomen of the female has several pairs (up to four) of dark tubercles ↑, often with small hairs. On the abdomen of the female, dark lines often connect the tubercles. The male is more drably colored. Females are 2 to 4 mm in length, while males are about 2 to 3 mm.

Web & Hunting Technique: This spider makes a 1/8th or 45 degree orb web. It consists of about four radial strands of silk with ten or more rows of connecting silk.

Life Cycle: Active in summer. Little is known of this spider's life cycle.

Range: Found throughout the Carolinas. The Triangle Weaver ranges from New England to Florida and west to Missouri.

Nature Notes:

The apex of the Triangle Weaver's web is usually attached to a branch where the small, brownish female sits, resembling a bud on the twig (see illustration below).

Actual size of adult female Triangle Weaver

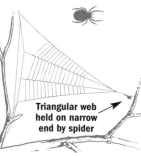

Triangular web held on narrow end by spider

Featherlegged Orbweaver *Uloborus glomosus*

Wide variety of habitats. It is common around houses but is also present in dry woods, floodplain woods and wood edges.

Nature Notes:

Uloborids are among the few spiders that do not have poison glands.

Immatures of *Uloborus glomosus* are known to make communal webs.

Actual size of adult female Featherlegged Orbweaver

Description: Also known as the Hackled Web Orbweaver, this spider is another cribellate spider. It is so named because of the presence of a clump of long, brush-like hairs ↑ on the extremely long (over four times the length of the cephalothorax) Leg I of the female. The spider is brownish to gray and color and is rarely seen outside of its web. It has a pronounced arched or "hump"-backed abdomen. Females are 3 to 5 mm in length, while males are about 2 to 3 mm long.

Web & Hunting Technique: This spider makes a rough orb web, but it is not a true orbweaver. Evidently the orb web has evolved twice in spiders. The female makes a small (up to about 10 inches in diameter) horizontal orb web, where it sits upside down. When disturbed, the spider holds all of its legs straight out in the same plane, resembling a twig (see *Tetragnatha* spp.).

Extremely long leg pair number 1 (Leg I) also sport brush-like hairs that give this spider its common name.

The female catches prey in her web; little is known of the male of this species—I have never seen one.

Life Cycle: It is often seen in May or June; therefore, it probably overwinters as a subadult and matures by June or July.

Range: Found throughout the Carolinas, the Featherlegged Orbweaver ranges from Canada to Florida and west to Nebraska.

Here is another angle of this strange looking spider.

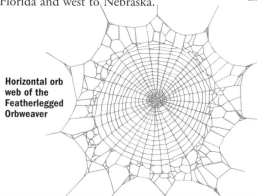

Horizontal orb web of the Featherlegged Orbweaver

Cobweb Weavers (Combfooted Spiders)
Family Theridiidae

Description
The cobweb weavers are also called the "combfooted spiders." The abdomen in most species in this family curves downward (anteriorly) and comes to a point at the spinnerets.

Similar Spiders
The theridiid spiders have a "comb" or set of bristles on the tarsus of Leg IV, a fact that separates them from the closely-related sheetweb weavers (Family Linyphiidae).

Habitat
Woods, meadows, houses, cities—spiders of this large family are found nearly everywhere.

Hunting Techniques/Web
The cobweb weavers make a chaotic web and hang upside down. When prey are caught in the web, the spider wraps and often carries it to a preferred portion of the web before eating it.

Diversity (Species Richness/Range)
Approximately 180 species of this family are found in North America. In South Carolina, over 45 cobweb weavers are known (Gaddy and Morse, 1985). Coyle (2008) lists 52 species for the Smokies. In both states combined there are over 60 species.

Cobweb Weavers (Family Theridiidae)

Cobweb typical of the Theridiidae

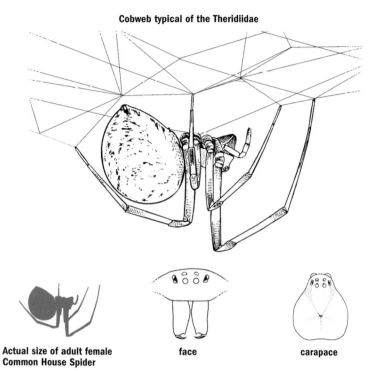

**Actual size of adult female
Common House Spider**

face

carapace

Common House Spider *Achaearanea tepidariorum*

F

M

Found primarily in man-made structures.

Nature Notes:

If left alone, the Common House Spider can be a helpful household exterminator. They catch roaches, flies, crickets and other small insects and invertebrates. I have even seen Carolina Scorpions in their webs!

Description: Also called the Domestic Spider, American House Spider or simply the House Spider, it is found in nearly every house, barn and man-made building. The female is brown to gray and often has darker chevrons on the abdomen with white lines ↑. It is very similar in appearance to *Tidarren sisyphoides* (the "Sisyphus Spider"), which is more common outdoors. Females 5 to 6 mm; males 3.8 to 4.7 mm.

Web & Hunting Technique: This is the spider that constructs the "cobwebs" that clutter up the corners of our rooms, our closets and under tables and chairs. The female sits upside down in the middle of the complex cobweb. The male occasionally appears in the web with her to mate.

Egg Sac & Eggs: The eggs sacs are dull gray to brown and teardrop-shaped. The female usually sits on the egg sac until the spiderlings hatch and disperse.

Even crickets are not safe from the cobwebs of the Common House Spider.

Life Cycle: Active year round.

Range: They are common all over the Carolinas and are found across Canada and the United States.

Note the dark and white chevrons on the abdomen.

A good look at the dorsum (top side) of the American House Spider.

Nephila Dewdrop Spider *Argyrodes nephilae*

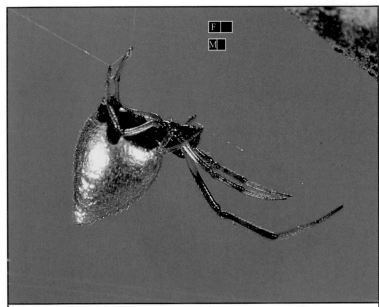

Woodlands. Found in the webs of orbweaver spiders.

Nature Notes:

These spiders are known to be kleptoparasites or inquilines, living off food debris in the large webs of larger spiders. I have, however, seen *Argyrodes trigonum* in the small webs of the Bowl-and-Doily Spider and the Filmy Dome Spider.

Six species of *Argyrodes*, the dewdrop spiders, are known from the Carolinas (and another species' range overlaps the state) (Gaddy and Morse, 1985). Of these, only *A. trigonum* and *A. nephilae* are common.

Description: *Argyrodes nephilae* is the smallest of the three Carolina species and has a rounded triangular abdomen. *Argyrodes trigonum* is a brownish spider with a triangular abdomen, whose tip is often slightly curved. The Dewdrop Spider is chrome-colored, however, and can easily be spotted in the webs of large orbweavers, where it appears to be a drop of quicksilver. Females 2 to 3 mm; males 1 to 2 mm.

Web & Hunting Technique: These species catch or eat their prey in webs. *A. nephilae* lives off the debris from leftover food in orbweaver webs. *A. trigonum* makes a small web or can live in the webs of larger spiders. *A. nephilae* usually lives in the webs of orbweavers, particularly *Nephila clavipes*, from whom it gets its specific name.

Egg Sac & Eggs: The egg sac of *A. trigonum* is a distinctive bell-shaped sac with a pointed tip. It hangs from twigs on a thin thread.

Argyrodes spiders are kleptoparasites—living in the webs of larger spiders (especially orb-weavers) where they feed on food missed or cast off by the larger spider.

Life Cycle: These spiders are active in early summer and probably overwinter as subadults.

Range: *Argyrodes nephilae* is a tropical species that was not thought to range much farther north than *Nephila clavipes,* in whose web it is usually found. In 2006, however, I found an *A. nephilae* in the web of *Araneus bicentenarius* in the mountains of South Carolina—it is also now reported from Arkansas (Dorris, 1968). It probably ranges up the North Carolina coast to the Outer Banks. *A. trigonum,* which is more common and widespread than *A. nephilae,* is found throughout the Carolinas and all over Canada and the United States.

A finger gives us scale to help visualize how tiny these spiders really are.

Brown Widow *Latrodectus geometricus*

F

M

Houses and other man-made structures.

Nature Notes:

Dr. Robert Wolff, a South Carolina arachnologist, thinks the Brown Widow is moved around in cargo shipped via 18-wheeler trucks.

ALL WIDOWS ARE VENOMOUS AND ARE DANGEROUS SPIDERS; HOWEVER, THESE SPIDERS GENERALLY DO NOT BITE UNLESS YOU ENTER THEIR WEB.

Description: The Brown Widow is not black at all and resembles the American House Spider somewhat. It has an orangeish hourglass ↑ on the ventral portion of the abdomen. Females 5 to 10 mm long, males 3 to 5 mm.

Web & Hunting Technique: The widows occupy large cobwebs and invariably sit upside down in the center of the web, especially at night.

Egg Sac & Eggs: Eggs sacs are up to 25 mm in diameter and are guarded by the female. She usually deposits the egg sac a considerable distance away from the web.

Life Cycle: In man-made structures, Brown Widows are active year round.

Range: The Brown Widow, which has just recently become common in the Carolinas (it was not even mentioned in Gaddy and Morse, 1985), is slowly advancing from its southern tropical source.

Southern Black Widow *Latrodectus mactans*

F

M

Buildings: basements, outbuildings, barns, houses.

Description: This is the widow of basements, houses and out-buildings. Females have the distinctive bright red "hourglass" ↑ on the venter of the abdomen. Females 5 to 10 mm long, males 3 to 5 mm.

Web & Hunting Technique: The widows occupy large cobwebs and invariably sit upside down in the center of the web, especially at night.

Egg Sac & Eggs: Eggs sacs ↑ are up to 25 mm in diameter and are guarded by the female. She usually deposits the egg sac a considerable distance away from the web.

Life Cycle: In man-made structures, Widows are active year round. In the wild, black widows overwinter as subadults under leaf litter or debris. Unlike most spiders (which mature in the late summer or fall), black widows mature in May and June in the Carolinas.

Range: The Southern Black Widow is more common in the Coastal Plain of the Carolinas.

Nature Notes:

Black widow males generally do not make webs; they are most commonly seen in the spring when they appear in and around the webs of females.

ALL WIDOWS ARE VENOMOUS AND ARE DANGEROUS SPIDERS; HOWEVER, THESE SPIDERS GENERALLY DO NOT BITE UNLESS YOU ENTER THEIR WEB.

The notorious 'hourglass' is found under the abdomen.

Northern Black Widow *Latrodectus variolus*

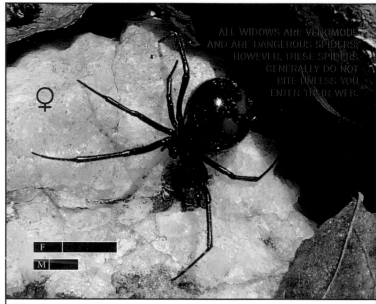

ALL WIDOWS ARE VENOMOUS AND ARE DANGEROUS SPIDERS; HOWEVER, THESE SPIDERS GENERALLY DO NOT BITE UNLESS YOU ENTER THEIR WEB.

♀

F

M

Woods.

Nature Notes:

Males are small, long-legged and more brightly colored than the females.

Despite the prevailing mythology, males are not always eaten by the female after mating.

Description: Females show red spots above and have two red triangles or the "broken hourglass pattern" on the underside of the abdomen. Females 5 to 10 mm long, males 3 to 5 mm.

Web & Hunting Technique: The large web (over one meter high) has a funnel tube connecting it to a retreat on the ground under leaf litter. During the day, the female stays in the retreat, at night she appears in the middle of the cobweb.

Egg Sac & Eggs: Eggs sacs are guarded by the female. She usually deposits the egg sac a considerable distance away from the web.

Life Cycle: In the wild, black widows overwinter as subadults under leaf litter or debris. They mature in May and June in the Carolinas.

Range: It is more common in the Piedmont and Mountains. The Northern Black Widow is found from Canada and New England south to Florida and west to Oklahoma.

Lizard Spider *Rhomphaea fictilium (=Argyrodes f.)*

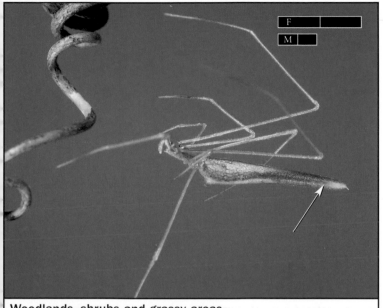

Woodlands, shrubs and grassy areas.

Description: The strange, spectacular spider is one of the largest of the small "dewdrop spiders," as most of the small *Argyrodes* are called. It is light brown to yellowish with scattered chrome and silvery markings, but is usually identified by its shape not its color. The abdomen is extended beyond the spinnerets several millimeters. The abdomen becomes extremely long ↑. Females 10 to 13 mm long. Males to 5mm.

Web & Hunting Technique: The Lizard Spider is generally found in its own small web.

Life Cycle: These spiders are active in early summer and probably overwinter as subadults.

Range: *R. fictilium* is found sporadically in the Carolinas. Reported from the Great Smoky Mountains National Park (Coyle 1985) to South Carolina's barrier islands (Gaddy and Morse, 1985). It ranges from Canada to Argentina.

Nature Notes:

The Lizard Spider has been alternatively called *Rhomphaea fictilium* or *Argyrodes fictilium* by taxonomists.

This spider is easily overlooked.

Though the Lizard Spider makes its own web, most of its close relatives are known to be kleptoparasites or inquilines, living off food debris in the webs of larger spiders.

False Black Widow *Steatoda grossa*

Found around houses, under boards, in barns and habitats similar to those of the Brown Widow and Southern Black Widow.

Nature Notes:

At least four other species of *Steatoda* are found in the Carolinas (Gaddy and Morse, 1985).

This spider has been known to live up to six years.

Description: The False Black Widow is dark spider ranging in color from dirty beige to purplish black. The darker individuals are often mistaken for the Southern Black Widow. The abdomen is shaped similar to black widows, with ventral spinnerets and a pointed abdomen. No hourglass markings or red spots, however, are present on the abdomen of the False Black Widow. Females 6 to 10 mm long; males 4 to 7 mm.

Web & Hunting Technique: The females make a small cobweb; I have never seen a male.

Egg Sac & Eggs: Eggs sacs are smaller than those of *Latrodectus* species.

Life Cycle: Not known.

Range: The False Black Widow is found throughout the Carolinas. Found in the coastal states of the Atlantic, Gulf and Pacific regions, according to Kaston (1978).

Leafy Cobweb Weaver *Theridion frondeum*

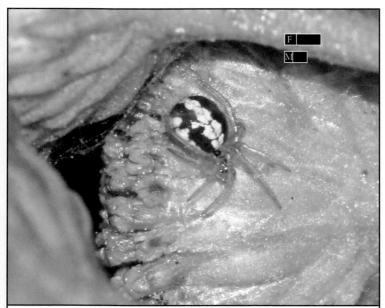

F ▮▮▮
M ▮▮▮

Swamps, floodplains, upland Piedmont woods, mesic mountain woods, barrier islands and houses.

Description: *Theridion frondeum* has a yellow abdomen marked with two brown scalloped stripes. Caution: There is wide variation in the abdomen pattern! The abdomen is oval-shaped, with the spinnerets on the undersides. The tarsal portion of Leg IV has a distinct comb-shaped array of bristles (often not visible with the naked eye). Female 2 to 4 mm long; male 1 to 3 mm.

Web & Hunting Technique: This species is in the cobweb weaver family and makes a small chaotic cobweb in trees, shrubs, grassy fields and in dwellings.

Egg Sac & Eggs: Small, white spheres approximately 5 mm in diameter.

Life Cycle: Probably overwinter as immatures; matures in mid-summer.

Range: These species occur in all physiographic provinces of the Carolinas. Most of the species in this genus are found primarily in eastern North America.

Nature Notes:

There are 11 species of *Theridion* reported from South Carolina and 15 species, including one new to science, known from the Smokies in North Carolina (Coyle 2008).

Webs of Theridiid spiders are complex cobwebs in tops of shrubs and grasses.

Sheetweb Weavers
Family Linyphiidae (Subfamily Linyphiinae)

Description
The sheetweb weavers are known for their bow- or dome-shaped webs. They are small spiders with spiny legs and bodies rarely longer than 10 mm. They hang upside down under sheet webs.

Similar Spiders
Cobweb weavers (theridiid spiders) have larger, fatter abdomens and do not have spines on the legs.

Habitat
Forests and meadows; only rarely found near buildings or disturbed areas.

face   carapace

Hunting Techniques/Web
These spiders are rarely found outside of their sheet webs. They cling upside down below their dome- or bowl-shaped web, which is hung from grasses or low shrubs by a complex system of threads.

Diversity (Species Richness/Range
There are approximately 250 species of this family in North America. A northern family, 36 species, including ten new species, are found in the Smokies of North Carolina (Coyle 2008). In South Carolina, less than 10 species are linyphiids are known (Gaddy and Morse, 1985).

Sheetweb Weavers (Family Linyphiidae)

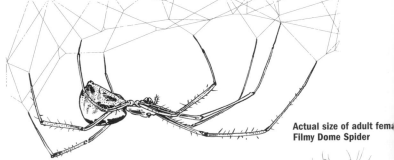

**Actual size of adult fema
Filmy Dome Spider**

Sheetweb weavers usually hang inverted below sheet-like webs

Scarlet Spider *Florinda coccinea*

Nearly always found near the ground in low grasses.

Description: The Scarlet Spider is a small, bright red spider. Also called the Red Grass Spider, it is rarely yellowish to orange. Most spiders, however, are completely scarlet except for the eye mound ↑ and a tubercle on the tip of the abdomen ↑, both of which are black. Female and male 3 mm long.

Web & Hunting Technique: It makes a small, flat web a few inches off of the ground in grass. The web sags here and there and looks like a loosely-hung sheet of cloth. The spider walks upside down on the underside of the web. When the dew is heavy, this web holds extremely large drops of dew.

Life Cycle: Unknown; usually most commonly seen in late summer and fall.

Range: Locally common in the Carolinas. Ranges north to Maryland, south to Florida and west to Texas and Illinois.

Nature Notes:

The low webs of the Scarlet Spider hold large drops of dew (see photo below).

Scarlet Spiders cling to the undersides of their webs.

Bowl-and-Doily Spider *Frontinella pyramitela*

F ███
M ██

Wood edges, shrubby areas, pastures and natural grasslands.

Nature Notes:

The best time to appreciate the beauty of the Bowl-and-Doily Spider is on a dewy, late summer or fall morning, when fields and roadsides are often covered with hundreds of their webs.

Description: The Bowl-and-Doily Spider is rarely found outside of its distinctive web (see image below right) and is usually quickly identified by its web, not its body shape. The male is mostly brown with few markings. The female is brown with white stripes on either side of the abdomen ↑ and sometimes shows yellow spots on the lower side of the abdomen. The female is 3 to 5 mm, while the male is 3 to 3.5 mm long.

Web & Hunting Technique: The "bowl" is placed directly over (and connected to) a flatter web called the "doily." The female is usually found in or under the bowl portion of the web; the male appears in the web in late summer and fall.

Life Cycle: Active from May through October in the Carolinas.

Range: Common throughout the Carolinas. Found throughout the United States.

The only way to get this view is to be lying on your back! Bowl-and-Doily Spiders spend most of their time clinging upside down to the undersides of their web.

Males are smaller and drabber than females.

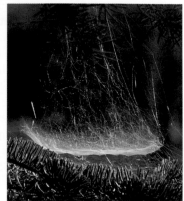

The web that gives this spider its name. The bowl is obvious but the 'doily' is partially hidden by the branch.

Filmy Dome Spider *Neriene radiata*

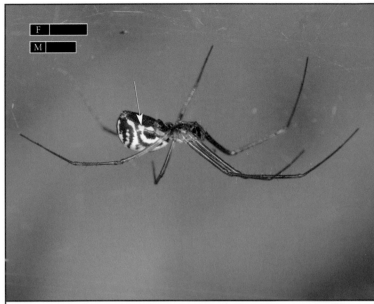

F

M

Variety of habitats including shrubby areas. This species is more common in woodlands than the Bowl-and-Doily Spider.

Nature Notes:

This spider web is most easily appreciated on dewy fall mornings.

The Basilica Spider, an orbweaver, also makes a dome, but it is an orb web that has been pulled upward by a lifting thread and not a true dome.

Description: The Filmy Dome Spider, another sheetweb weaver, is also known by its web. Both the female and the male have more white on their bodies than do the Bowl-and-Doily Spider. The female is mostly silvery white with a brown stripe extending the length of the body. She shows yellow dashes that connect to white stripes ↑ on the sides of the abdomen. The male is predominantly brown with parallel white stripes on the sides of its abdomen. The female is 4 to 6 mm, while the male is 3 to 5 mm long.

Web & Hunting Technique: Both male and female are often found upside down in the fine-webbed "dome" for which this species is known. There is a large, complex system of threads above the dome where most of the prey is caught. Victims then drop down to the dome or are brought there by the spider.

The web does look like a 'filmy dome.' The webs become very visible on dewy mornings.

Life Cycle: Active from May through October in the Carolinas.

Range: Common throughout the Carolinas. Found in most of the United States.

A Filmy Dome Spider has captured a meal.

Longjawed Orbweavers
Family Tetragnathidae

Description

The longjawed orbweavers are
known for their long, thin bodies and extremely long legs.

Similar Spiders

The cellar spiders have
even longer legs and are
most commonly
encountered indoors.

Habitat

Forests and openings, usually along the margins of bodies
of water or near water.

orb-style web;
note open hub

Hunting Techniques/Web

The longjawed orbweavers build an
open orb web with few radii. They hunt
from the web at night and remain camouflaged by
day by folding their legs in a single plane and resting on twigs.

Observations

Spiders of this family can walk on the surface tension of
water; occasionally, they can be seen "running" across
water using a cartwheel-like movement of the legs. They
are frequently found in boats mooring along the margins of
rivers and lakes.

Diversity (Species Richness/Range)

About 25 species of this family are found in North
America. In the Carolinas, about 10 species are known to
occur (Gaddy and Morse, 1985).

Typical
longjawed
orbweaver

Longjawed Orbweavers
(Family Tetragnathidae)

face

Nephilid Orbweavers
Family Nephilidae

Description

The nephilid orbweavers are known for their giant abdomens, long, bristle-covered legs (Legs I, II, and IV) and bright body colors. Their abdomens are less rounded than true orb-weavers, sometimes being several centimeters long (20-60 cm). Males are diminutive, often being only one-tenth the size of females.

Similar Spiders

None.

Habitat

Primarily forests, forest edges and openings in forests.

Golden Silk Orbweaver

Hunting Techniques/Web

Most species of this family make large, yellowish or "golden" webs. The webs are extremely sticky and are used to make small fishing nets by primitive people in New Guinea. Each web (some over one meter wide) has a female, sometimes over ten males, and various species of inquiline spiders (usually of the genus *Argyrodes*), who survived on small insects the female and males do not eat.

Eggs Sacs and Eggs

The egg sacs are rounded to oval-shaped and are placed on nearby limbs and twigs. Nephilid orbweavers are noteworthy in that they are often triple-brooded, producing three egg sacs per year.

Diversity (Species Richness/Range)

This is a tropical family with about 25 species worldwide. Our one species, *Nephila clavipes*, ranges south into South America.

Nephilid Orbweavers (Family Nephilidae)

Page 72   Golden Silk Orbweaver (*Nephila clavipes*)

Orchard Orbweaver *Leucage venusta*

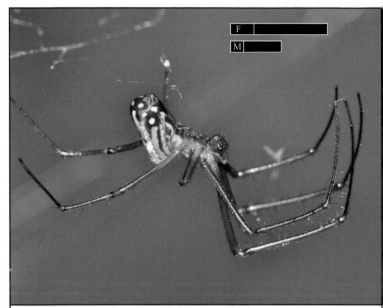

F ▮▮▮▮▮▮▮▮▮▮
M ▮▮▮▮▮

Mixed hardwood forests. Moist woods (coves in Appalachians, floodplain forests). Sometimes even found in orchards!

Nature Notes:

From a distance, the silvery stripes and the red spots first capture the viewer's eye. The spider sits upside down in a near-horizontal web, exhibiting the red spot(s) of its abdomen's tip and its underside.

In fall and in winter on warm days, immature Orchard Orbweavers are often seen in the leaf litter or on tree bark in moist mixed hardwood forests.

Description: A beautiful, colorful orbweaver. The dorsum of the abdomen has a complex pattern of silver, yellow, green and black. The venter (underside) of the abdomen is black with one central, horseshoe-shaped red marking ↑ and two smaller red or reddish-orange spots near the tip (also visible from the dorsal side of the abdomen). The female is 5.5 to 7.5 mm in length; the male is 3.5 to 4.0 mm.

Web & Hunting Technique: Diurnal orb-web hunter.

Egg Sac & Eggs: It is reported that the egg sacs of the Orchard Orbweaver are made of "orange-white" silk (Jackman, 1991).

Life Cycle: Overwinters as a subadult and matures in late spring and early summer.

Range: Eastern United States. Common in spring in mixed hardwood forests in all provinces of the Carolinas.

We most often see the undersides and sides of this spider as it waits for prey beneath its web. But as the photo shows above, the top side is equally attractive.

The red horseshoe-shaped mark on the spiders undersides are what most observers first notice.

Nature Notes:

Gaddy (1987) found the Orchard Orbweaver the most abundant orbweaver in a rich cove forest in the southern Appalachians of South Carolina in May and June, when the spider usually matures. And in Congaree Swamp, a large floodplain in the Coastal Plain of South Carolina, the Orchard Orbweaver was again the most dominant orbweaver in April, May and June (Wharton et al., 1981). It is also quite common in the maritime forests of the Outer Coastal Plain in early spring (Gaddy, 1981).

Longjawed Orbweaver species *Tetragnatha* spp.

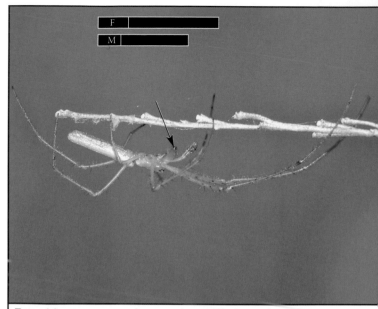

F

M

Found in grasses, sedges and cattails in and near water. Occasionally found in low grasses quite a distance from water.

Nature Notes:

If you have ever boated along a small river or canoed in a lake, chances are you have seen a longjawed orbweaver in your boat. They build webs in unoccupied boats and drop from twigs into boats when disturbed.

Coyle (2008) reports four common species Tetragnatha and a new, yet unnamed species, from the Smokies.

Longjawed orbweavers can walk or run on the surface tension of water. When running, they move their legs in a cartwheel fashion and appear to be "rolling" across the water.

Description: Four *Tetragnatha* species are common in the Carolinas. As their names indicate, the longjawed orbweavers have extended "jaws" (chelicerae) ↑. In the males of *T. elongata*, for example, the chelicerae are longer than the cephalothorax. In the other species, the chelicerae are from one-half as long to almost the same length as the jaws. All species of *Tetragnatha* have long legs and slender bodies.

Silver Longjawed Orbweaver (*Tetragnatha laboriosa*): Abdomen silvery gray with small yellow spots, slight bulge near middle; females 6 mm in length, males 5 mm long.

Elongate Stilt Orbweaver (*Tetragnatha elongata*): Abdomen gray with yellow-brown markings, very thin, no bulge; females 9 mm in length, males 8 mm long.

Manycolored Longjawed Orbweaver (*Tetragnatha versicolor*): Abdomen gray to black, thin, often with silvery stripe; females

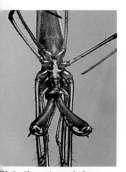

Note the extremely long chelicerae (jaws) of this species.

This is the longjawed orbweavers first line of defense — look like a piece of grass.

The red "appendages" on this spider are actually parasitic mites.

about 7 mm in length, males 5 mm.

Strawcolored Longjawed Orbweaver (*Tetragnatha straminea*): Abdomen dull yellow-brown to gray; with silvery border; females 8 mm long , males 6 to 7 mm.

Web & Hunting Technique:

They build an open orb web with fewer radial lines than the true orbweavers (family Araneidae). Their webs are usually vertically-oriented. The spider is rarely seen in the web by day; it is usually camouflaged (by folding in its legs) on a nearby twig.

Tetragnatha webs have open hubs. Note the lack of spirals in the web's center.

Egg Sac & Eggs: Subglobose (in *T. versicolor*), 5 to 6 mm long, 60 to 100 eggs.

Life Cycle: Matures from March until late fall, probably overwinters as spiderling or subadult.

Range: *T. laboriosa* and *T. elongata* are found throughout the continental U. S., Canada and ato Alaska. *T. versicolor* is found throughout e U.S. and *T. straminea* is found primarily in tern U.S.

Actual size of a female longjawed orbweaver

Golden Silk Orbweaver *Nephila clavipes*

Common in barrier island live oak forests. Inland, it seems to prefer open upland and floodplain woods.

Nature Notes:

There is one record of a dead Eastern Towhee being found in the web of a Golden Silk Orbweaver in Georgia.

In New Guinea, the webs of a species of *Nephila* are used to make fishing nets (see drawing in Hillyard, 1994).

Sometimes called the Banana Spider in southern Georgia and Florida.

Actual size of adult female Golden Silk Orbweaver

Description: One of the largest North American orbweavers. In the Carolinas, the female's body may be as long as 45 mm, and usually ranges from 20-40 mm. The abdomen is bright yellow and curved, resembling a fat banana (and prompting one of the spider's common names). The female has distinctive tufts of long, spiny hairs on legs I, II and IV ↑. The male is diminutive, often only one-tenth the size of the female, and a nondescript wine-brown color.

Web & Hunting Technique: The female is diurnal and never seen outside of the giant web, which may be six feet across! The webs are golden yellow, strong and very sticky. In addition to one female and many males, the web is often occupied by several other species of small spiders, especially those in the genus *Argyrodes*. These tiny "kleptoparasites" forage in the web and eat things too small for the

Golden Silk females and males. On the Carolina barrier islands, the Nephila Dewdrop Spider (*Argyrodes nephilae*) with its glittering chrome body, is conspicuous in the webs of the Golden Silk and gets its specific name from its association with *Nephila clavipes*.

Egg Sac & Eggs: Along the Outer Coastal Plain on barrier islands, Golden Silk females often produce three egg sacs per year. The egg sac is papery brown and is placed on a twig or limb near the nest.

Life Cycle: In late summer, males (I have counted as many as 12) enter the female's web and jockey for position to be the first to mate with her. Being only a fraction her size, they must be careful not to be eaten by the female. For safety's sake, the males often approach the female and mate with her while she is eating a large insect or during her last molt (if this is the first mating) (some species of *Nephila* molt 14 times before becoming a full-sized adult). The female often hangs from a drying thread in the center of the web after her final molt. I have seen a male climb down the thread and mate with her. The female appears to live only one year in the Carolinas. In the tropics, it probably lives several years. Males live only a few weeks.

Range: This is a neotropical species, ranging from Amazonian South America up the Carolina coast just into North Carolina. Although primarily found on barrier islands in South Carolina, it occasionally ranges inland, traveling up major river floodplains such as the Savannah and the Santee/Congaree. The spider appears to have increased its northern and inland range in the last few decades (global warming?). The genus *Nephila* also occurs in the Old World tropics.

...s of the Golden ...aver.

The tiny male approaches the huge female in the web.

Note the brush-like hairs on the femur and tibia.

Orbweavers
Family Araneidae

Description

The orbweavers are known for their large abdomens, which are often twice to three times as large as the cephalothorax. The abdomen in the orbweavers also takes on many strange shapes; there are star-shaped abdomens, spiny abdomens, crab-shaped abdomens, etc. They have eight eyes and spiny legs.

Similar Spiders

Tetragnathids and uloborids also make orb webs, but the spiders of these families are very different in appearance from true orbweavers.

Habitat

Forests, savannahs, meadows, old fields and near structures, but rarely, if ever, in houses.

Hunting Techniques/Web

The most distinctive feature of this family is, of course, the orb web. It consists of circular sticky lines with radii (non-sticky) emanating out from the webs center. The webs are usually vertical and are often taken down (eaten) in the morning and re-erected at night. The spider waits for prey in the center of the web or in a nearby retreat, connected to the web by a "telegraph" thread.

Eggs Sacs and Eggs

The egg sacs of the orbweavers are, on the whole, oval- or teardrop-shaped. They usually contain thousands of eggs and are placed on twigs and limbs away from the web. Most orbweavers produce one egg sac per year, but some species are multi-brooded.

Diversity (Species Richness/Range)

There over 120 species of orbweavers in North America. In South Carolina, there are around 60 species of orbweavers known (Gaddy and Morse, 1985). In both states combined there may be as many as 75 species.

Orbweavers (Family Araneidae)

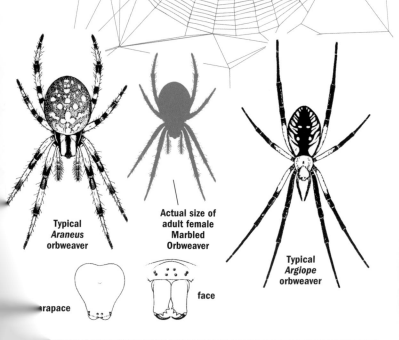

Typical
Araneus
orbweaver

Actual size of
adult female
Marbled
Orbweaver

Typical
Argiope
orbweaver

arapace

face

Difoliate Orbweaver *Acacesia hamata*

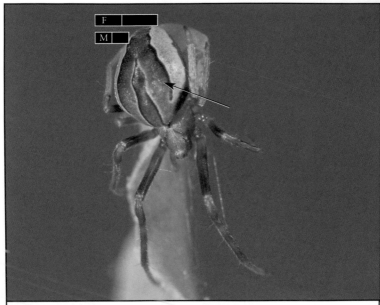

Forest openings, grassy and shrubby areas.

Nature Notes:

Gaddy and Morse (1985) reported that they caught several *Acacesia hamata* individuals in a grassy field sweep netting for jumping spiders. They also surmised that because they did not see the spider's web, it may be nocturnal or build extremely low webs.

Description: The Difoliate Orbweaver is a grayish-brown small to medium-sized orbweaver with very distinctive abdominal markings. The dorsum of the rhombic-shaped abdomen has a large brown band that tapers toward its end; within that band, a darker brown, smaller, pointed band extends half the abdomen's length ↑. Both bands are outlined with darker brown lines. Spines are present on the legs and are especially prominent in males. The female is 4.7 to 9.1 mm in length; the male is 3.6 to 5.0 mm.

Web & Hunting Technique: Howell and Jenkins (2004) noted that the Difoliate Orbweaver builds a 8 to 12 inch web three to four feet off the ground and is nocturnal.

Life Cycle: Not known.

Range: Eastern United States to Texas an Illinois. Found throughout the Carolinas

Starbellied Orbweaver *Acanthepeira stellata*

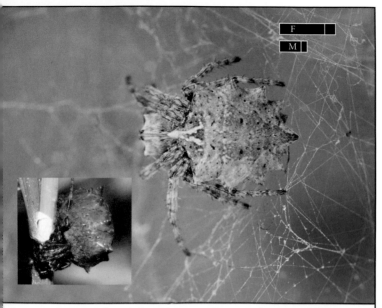

Forests, forest edges, shrubby openings and grassy fields.

Description: A unique orbweaver with prominent spikes or tubercles on its abdomen, giving the spider the shape of a star. The distal tip of the abdomen often has a darker chevron pattern coming to a point, and there is sometimes a white triangle on a spike that extends over the cephalothorax. The abdomen and the cephalothorax are brown to grayish. The female is 11 to 12 mm long; male 6 to 7 mm.

Web & Hunting Technique: The female sits head-down in a large orb web and is known to quickly drop from the web upon being disturbed.

Egg Sac & Eggs: Egg sac is a "mass of loose, brown silk, attached to a leaf" (Kaston, 1948).

Life Cycle: Overwinters as a subadult and matures in the spring and early summer. Gaddy (1981) found mature adults in May and June on South Carolina's barrier islands.

Range: Eastern United States. Found throughout the Carolinas.

Nature Notes:

In the Carolinas, *Acanthepeira stellata* may be confused with three rarer species of *Acanthepeira* (see Levi, 1976 for taxonomy).

This female will spin a new web after dark to replace this damaged one.

Giant Orbweaver *Araneus bicentenarius*

Forests and forest edges.

Nature Notes:

The Giant Orbweaver is the largest of the angulate, or large, *Araneus* orbweavers. The only orbweavers comparable in body size to this giant are the Golden Silk Orbweaver (*Nephila clavipes*), the Marbled Orbweaver (*Araneus marmoreus*), the Tree Orbweaver (*Araneus gemma*), the Shamrock Orbweaver (*Araneus trifolium*) and the Cross Orbweaver (*Araneus diadematus*). The latter three species generally rare or absent in the Carolinas.

(continued on next page)

Description: The Giant Orbweaver is the largest of what Levi (1971) calls the "large" *Araneus* orbweavers. It is a beautiful spider: its large, fat abdomen is dark green to lichen-gray with black and brown background colors. Two large black and white "humps" ↑ are found on the spider's abdomen just above the cephalothorax. Near the tip of the abdomen, a black-lined chevron pattern is conspicuous. The legs are black and white with reddish-brown markings. Females in the Carolinas range from 20 mm to 30 mm in length and can be up to 20 mm in width just before the eggs are deposited. The male is reportedly less than 10 mm.

Web & Hunting Technique: At night, this spider builds a web three to four feet in diameter and hides in a leaf (or camouflages on lichens, mosses or Spanish moss—see below) retreat during the day. It keeps a "telegraph" line—a strand of silk from the middle of the web to the spider's leg—active during the da

Because of its greenish color, the Giant Orbweaver is often found on greenish-gray bark lichens or other green vegetation such as mosses or Spanish Moss.

to sense any prey in the web. To find the large female, one simply follows the telegraph line to the leaf retreat. If you shake the retreat gently, the spider will run out onto the web and can be observed or photographed.

Life Cycle: Overwinters as a subabult and matures early for such a large spider. In the Coastal Plain, this spider is mature by April, and in the Mountains, it is on the web by late May and early June. Usually any extremely large orb web encountered this time of year in the forests of the Carolinas is that of the Giant Orbweaver (the Golden Silk Orbweaver builds in late summer and fall; the Marbled Orbweaver is active only in the fall).

Range: Eastern North America from Nova Scotia to Florida (Levi, 1971). Many authors, including Levi (1971), consider this spider rare. 'n the Carolinas, it is locally common in ꞏoring and early summer.

(Nature Notes, continued)

Also called the "Lichen Spider" due to its propensity to camouflage on greenish-gray bark lichens.

In the Coastal Plain of South Carolina, it often makes a retreat in Spanish moss (*Tillandsia usneoides*), in which it is well camouflaged.

Redspotted Orbweaver *Araneus cingulatus*

Forests edges, shrubby openings. On barrier islands, this spider is common in maritime shrub zones near the beachfront.

Nature Notes:

The Redspotted Orbweaver is one of what Levi (1973) has called the 'small' *Araneus* orbweavers.

Description: The dorsum of the abdomen is green with two opposite lines of four small red spots surrounded by yellow ↑. Several red spots may also be found in the central area of the abdomen. The female is 4.6 to 6.0 mm long; the male is 2.7 to 3.5 mm.

Web & Hunting Technique: Makes a small orb web in the evening and usually hides in a retreat by day.

Life Cycle: Strangely, adults of this spider have been found in almost every season in the Carolinas.

Range: According to Levi (1973), this species is found from Massachusetts south to Florida and west to Missouri and Texas. It is found in the Mountains, Piedmont and Coastal Plain, but most commonly in the Coastal Plain.

Whitestriped Orbweaver *Araneus juniperi*

Peach orchards, Eastern Red Cedars.

Description: The Whitestriped Orbweaver is another of Levi's (1973) small *Araneus* orbweavers. The abdomen is greenish-yellow to yellowish with three distinct longitudinal white stripes on the dorsum. Occasionally, these stripes have red spots and are rarely red. The female is 2.5 to 5.2 mm long; the male is approximately 3.2 to 4.6 mm.

Web & Hunting Technique: Unknown.

Life Cycle: Adult males have been found in February in Florida, but most collections have been in spring and summer months.

Range: Nova Scotia to Florida and west to Arkansas and Texas, according to Levi (1973).

Nature Notes:

This spider has been found in peach orchards in South Carolina (Lee, 1981), but several collections, including one from a "cedar" glade in Arkansas, come from juniper trees [probably *Juniperus virginiana* (eastern red cedar)], hence the spider's specific name.

Marbled Orbweaver *Araneus marmoreus*

F

M

Forest, forest edges, shrubby openings.

Nature Notes:

The Marbled Orbweaver in the Carolinas is bright yellow and orange. As one goes north, this spider has darker pigment. In Canada and New England, near-black individuals are found.

Description: The Marbled Orbweaver is a large spider. The abdomen of the female (in the Carolinas) has a brownish-purple zigzag chevron pattern on a bright yellow or yellowish-orange background. (Farther north, the spider's abdomen is much darker, ranging from gray to almost black.) The front edge of the abdomen often shows best the marbling it is named for. The cephalothorax is reddish-brown to flesh-colored. Legs are ringed black and white ↑. Females are 9 to 18 mm long; males are 6 to 9 mm.

Web & Hunting Technique: The Marbled Orbweaver is typically found in a web along the edge of woods. It sits in its web by night and hides in a leaf retreat during the day. Like the Giant Orbweaver, it has a "signal" or "telegraph" line (while in the retreat) going from one of its legs to its orb. On cloudy days and in dark woods, the Marbled Orbweaver may occasionally be seen sitting in its web in the day.

A Marbled Orbweaver rests in its retreat. It is rarely seen until late in summer and autumn.

Life Cycle: The Marbled Orbweaver matures very late in the summer and into the autumn. Immatures are rarely seen. The spider is bright yellow and turns orange later in the season, usually towards late October; hence, its other common name in the South—the "Halloween" Spider. It is one of the few orbweavers that may be found as late as November.

Range: The Marbled Orbweaver is found in most of eastern North America and ranges north to Canada and on to Alaska and west to the Pacific Northwest. In the Carolinas, it is more common in the Mountains and Piedmont than in the Coastal Plain.

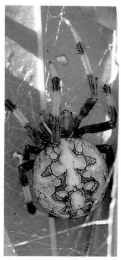

Also called the "Halloween Spider" as it turns more orange late in the season and can be found active in late October (and even into November).

Blackspotted Orbweaver *Araneus miniatus*

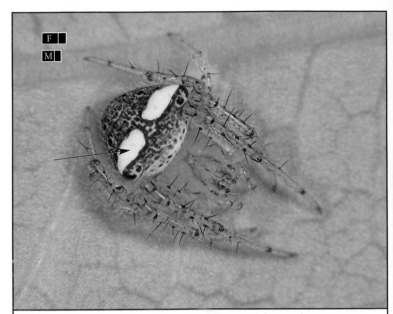

Barrier island maritime forests. Reported from citrus groves and Water Oak (*Quercus nigra*) forests in Florida by Levi (1973).

Nature Notes:

Reported from South Carolina barrier islands in Gaddy (1981) and listed as collected from Charleston County by Levi (1973).

Not uncommon in barrier island maritime forests in the Carolinas.

Description: The Blackspotted Orbweaver is a "small" *Araneus* orbweavers. The abdomen is triangular-shaped and has a yellowish-brown dorsum. Several black spots (usually four to six) are found on the dorsal posterior of the abdomen, two white bands occur near the dorsal anterior portion of the abdomen ↑. Occasionally, these bands are fused into one. The female is 3.0 to 4.7 mm long; the male is 2.5 to 3.7 mm.

Web & Hunting Technique: Unknown.

Life Cycle: Overwinters as an adult along the Carolina coast and in Florida.

Range: Found from Massachusetts south to northeastern Texas and Florida. Levi's (1973) map indicates that this spider is common along the Carolina coast.

Butterfly Orbweaver *Araneus pegnia*

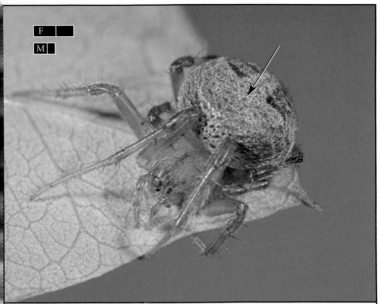

Forests edges, shrubby openings. On barrier islands, it is common in maritime shrub zones near the beach.

Description: The dorsum of the abdomen of this small colorful orbweaver is light to dark brown with two fused bright spots (ranging from pinkish to grayish in color) that form an inverted "butterfly" pattern ↑. The female is 4 to 8 mm long; the male is 2 to 5 mm.

Web & Hunting Technique: Makes a small orb web in the evening and usually hides in a retreat by day.

Life Cycle: Strangely, adults of this spider have been found in almost every season in South Carolina (Gaddy and Morse, 1985).

Range: According to Levi (1973), it is found in "bogs in Massachusetts to a river bottom in Costa Rica." In North America, it ranges from southern California northwesterly to Indiana. In the Carolinas, it is found in the Mountains, Piedmont and Coastal Plain, but most commonly in the Coastal Plain.

Nature Notes:

On my walks to the beach at Hunting Island State Park (Beaufort County, SC) in late January, I used to see individuals with bright pink butterfly patterns in the web or in small retreats. On other barrier islands, I have seen this spider with yellowish to whitish markings. Inland, the spider has yellow to gray markings.

Not all individuals are brightly marked.

Yellow Garden Spider *Argiope aurantia*

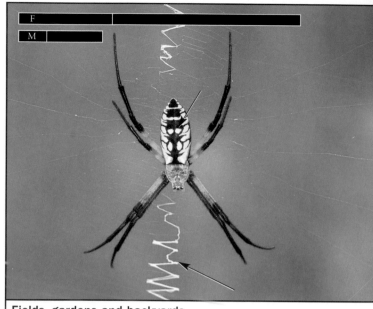

Fields, gardens and backyards.

Nature Notes:

The Yellow Garden Spider is well-known for its prey-wrapping methods. It often catches a large insect, paralyzes it with a bite to the back of the head, and then wraps it in thick silk for later consumption.

Sometimes the stabilimenta may have a repeated **W**-shaped pattern, prompting the old saying in the Coastal Plain of South Carolina that if the Writing Spider writes "war" or your name (that would be quite a feat—especially if you were named Elizabeth or William) while you are nearby, you will die soon.

Description: The Yellow Garden Spider, which is sometimes called the "Writing Spider," is a conspicuous orbweaver. The female's abdomen is bright yellow and black with several pairs of yellowish spots ↑, while its legs are paler yellow and black with long black spines. The cephalothorax (head) is covered with whitish hairs. The female ranges from 19 mm to 28 mm in length and her abdomen can be up to 20 mm in width just before she lays the egg sac in the fall. The male, which is rarely seen, is much smaller (5-8 mm) and duller in color.

Web & Hunting Technique: The Yellow Garden Spider makes a large (to 0.75 m across) web in open, non-forested areas. This spider is often called the "Writing Spider" in the South because of the white patterns in the center of its web. These silk zigzags ↑ are actually stabilimenta, web patterns that stabilize the central portion of the web and are thought to prevent

Immature females are not nearly as large or as brightly colored as mature females.

large insects from tearing the web apart when they fly into its center. (Recent studies, however, suggest that these stabilimenta may absorb ultraviolet rays in a way that would make them attractive to insects.)

Egg Sac & Eggs: The female builds a large spheroid egg sac with an urn-shaped opening and hangs it on nearby woody vegetation (usually a twig). In winter the egg sac is very conspicuous.

Life Cycle: Spiderlings emerge in late fall or spring. Adults mature in mid- to late summer.

Range: It is found from Canada to Costa Rica, according to Platnick (2007). In the Carolinas, it is common throughout the state.

The red spinnerets are very obvious on the undersides.

Banded Garden Spider *Argiope trifasciata*

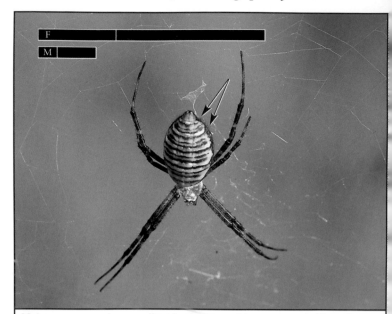

More common in woodland edges and in savannah-like sites—habitats too shady for the Yellow Garden Spider.

Nature Notes:

In the mountains of South Carolina, immatures of *A. trifasciata* are often found in the tubes of organ-pipe mud daubers (Gaddy and Morse, 1985).

Description: The Banded Garden Spider (or Banded Argiope) has yellow and black legs with black spines and a hirsute hairy cephalothorax like the more common Yellow Garden Spider; however, the abdomen of the Banded Garden Spider has thin alternating bands of black and yellow ↑ with four to six wider bands of creamy white. The females range from 15 mm to 25 mm in body length, while the males are from 4 mm to 5.5 mm. The male, when rarely seen, has an abdomen duller in coloration.

Web & Hunting Technique: Like the Yellow Garden Spider, the Banded Garden Spider also hangs upside down in its web. Its web usually lacks the large stabilimenta of the Yellow Garden Spider.

Egg Sac & Eggs: The egg sac of the Banded Garden Spider is flat-topped and sometimes resembles a half-globe.

Banded Garden Spiders can take very large prey. This female has wrapped up a good-sized grasshopper which she will eat later.

Life Cycle: *Argiope trifasciata* matures slightly earlier than *A. aurantia* (Gaddy, 1981).

Range: The Banded Garden Spider is generally cosmopolitan, but it is curiously absent from Europe. It is found throughout the Carolinas.

The Florida Garden Spider (*A. florida*) is found in the Sandhills of the Carolinas. It is uncommon in open longleaf pine (*Pinus palustris*) woods in South Carolina, being more common in central Florida scrub oak woodlands.

The yellow stripes and red spinnerets are very obvious on the undersides.

Conical Trashline Orbweaver *Cyclosa conica*

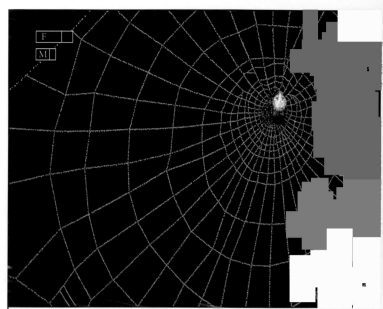

Open woodlands, light gaps in woods, woods edges. Shrubs in open areas from residential neighborhoods to forests.

Nature Notes:

If the web or the debris in the web is touched with a pointed object, the female will usually drop to the ground or move across the web.

Description: This strange spider has a long, pointed hump or tubercle protruding from the lower end of its abdomen. The abdomen of the female is dull gray and brown to nearly black in color. The female ranges from 5.3 to 7.5 mm in length; males are 3.6 to 4 mm.

Web & Hunting Technique: This orbweaver is a master of disguise. The female (the male is rarely seen) sits in the center of its web orienting her body in a straight line with pieces of leaves and old prey. Howell and Jenkins (2004), for this reason, called this species the Conical Trashline Orbweaver. She appears to be just another piece of debris and is overlooked by predators (and humans).

Life Cycle: Not known.

The 'trashline' referred to in this spider's common name is the row of bits of leaves and old prey down the center of the web.

Range: Found throughout the United States, Canada, Great Britain, Europe and the Middle East (Turkey). Locally common in the Carolinas.

Note the conical hump at the rear of the abdomen from which this spider gets its common name.

Humpbacked Orbweaver *Eustala anastera*

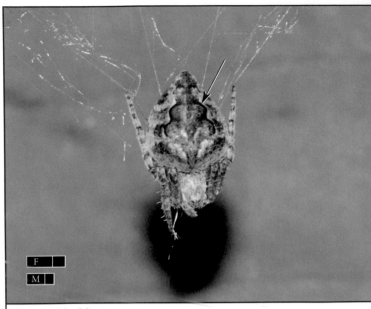

F ▢▢
M ▢▢

Forested habitats.

Nature Notes:

Eustala anastera is common in forested habitats, but its web is rarely seen. Comstock (1965) noted that the webs of this species are found in low shrubs.

The Humpbacked Orbweaver is a secretive spider of many variations in color and shade. The spider appears to be a master of camouflage. The beautiful green and gray lichen-colored form is usually seen in winter (I have frequently found them while cutting wood).

Description: Comstock (1965) gives an illustration of four typical color and pattern variations of the abdomen of females. Most females have brownish to gray abdomens with scattered hair. A scalloped-edged triangle outlined in black ↑ is often present on the abdomen. There is also greenish-gray variation occasionally seen in vegetation and a gray-black form often seen on lichens. *Eustala anastera* may actually be several species under one name. The female is 5 to 8 mm in length, while the male is 4 to 6 mm long. Males are rarely seen.

Web & Hunting Technique: The Humpbacked Orbweaver hunts in vertical webs found in low shrubs (Comstock, 1965).

Life Cycle: Often seen as an adult in winter. May overwinter under bark or leaf litter.

The green and gray form of the Humpbacked Orbweaver is often seen in winter. And the coloration makes it nearly invisible on lichen-covered branches.

Range: Found in eastern United States and Canada to the Rockies. Found throughout the Carolinas, though not abundant in any province.

Abdomen color can vary widely within the Humpbacked Orbweavers. The top spider is very brown and hardly resembles the green-marked individual (bottom). Look more at pattern and abdomen shape to identify this spider.

Spinybacked Orbweaver *Gasteracantha cancriform*

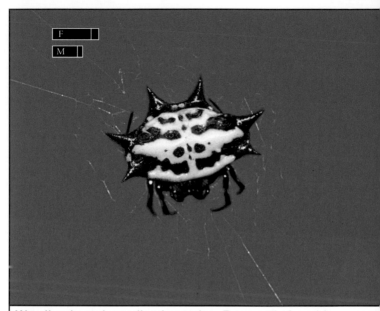

F

M

Woodlands and woodland margins. Frequently found in forested parks and backyards.

Nature Notes:

The female Spinybacked Orbweaver can be picked up by the spines (they exist to protect her from bird predation and do not sting) and examined. Because of the short length of the female's cephalothorax, she cannot reach your fingers with her fangs and, therefore, is unable to bite you.

I once held a female by her abdomen and let her cephalothorax rest on the back of my hand. She gently sank her fangs into my hand; I felt little or no pain at that moment. A small itchy bump appeared the next day.

Description: The Spinybacked Orbweaver, sometimes called the Crab Spider, is, as its name indicates, shaped like a crab with protruding spines scattered around its elliptically-shaped abdomen. This species is not a true crab spider (of the Thomisidae family), but is an orbweaver. The abdomen is white to yellowish to orange with dark spots and six black- or red-tipped spines. The cephalothorax is dark to black. The female's body may be over 10 mm wide and is about half as long as it is wide. The male is much smaller than the female and is rarely seen.

Web & Hunting Technique: The Spinybacked Orbweaver's web is very conspicuous up-close or from a distance. The web is very large (up to 50 cm in diameter) and has white bands of thick silk alternating on the major lines of its orb web. The female sits in the middle of the web in the daytime in an upside down position.

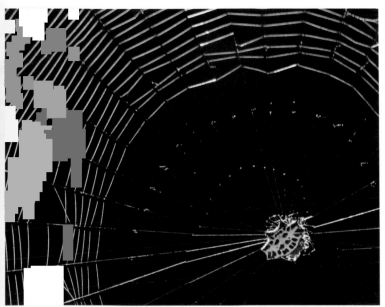

Webs of the *Gasteracantha* are things of beauty, especially when seen in backlighting. The sticky spiral threads are very close together.

Egg Sac & Eggs: In over twenty years of fieldwork in the Southeast, I have never seen the egg sac or the male of this species.

Life Cycle: Little is known of the life cycle of the Spinybacked Orbweaver. It matures in summer and sits in its web well into the autumn. Some individuals live until first frost

Range: This is a spider of the Coastal Plain. Kaston (1972) gives North Carolina as the species' northern range. I have seen this spider on the Outer Banks of North Carolina; it probably occurs in the Dismal Swamp in Virginia. It is rare in the Piedmont of the Carolinas. The Spinybacked Orbweaver is closely related to a host of strangely-shaped spinybacks from the tropics. Known from the Coastal Plain of southeastern United States west to California southward into the tropics. Found in the Coastal Plain and, rarely, in the lower Piedmont of the Carolinas.

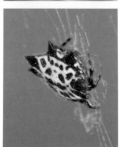

Color variations are common in the Spinybacked Orbweavers.

Seven-angled Orbweaver *Gea heptagon*

Wide variety of habitats—fields, grasslands, forests and open woods.

Nature Notes:

This strange orbweaver probably never has seven angles, but the abdomen of the female does have a strange shape, provoking its name.

It has also been called the Arrowhead Spider, but that name is usually reserved for *Verrucosa arenata*, a larger spider with an arrowhead shape on its abdomen.

Description: The abdomen is generally dark brown or yellowish-brown with a dark triangle near its tip ↑. A pair of prominent tubercles near the middle of the abdomen gives it an "angular" look. The female is 4.5 to 5.8 in length; the male is 2.6 to 4.3 mm. The male has prominent spines on its front legs.

Web & Hunting Technique: The small orb-web is found near the ground. The spider drops out of the web when disturbed and becomes darker in color in order to camouflage itself in the brown leaf litter (Sabath, 1969).

Egg Sac & Eggs: Ivory-colored, flattened with 30 to 45 eggs (Howell and Jenkins, 2004).

Life Cycle: Not known.

Range: Found north to New Jersey and Michigan, west to California. Common but not abundant throughout the Carolinas.

Basilica Orbweaver *Mecynogea lemniscata*

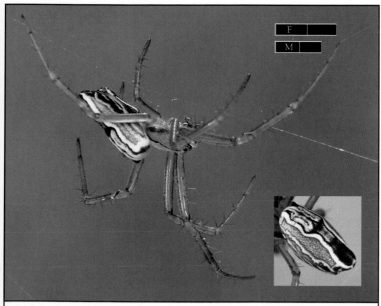

Deciduous forests and forest openings.

Description: Alternating bands of yellow, brown and white on the abdomen and a bright green and white pattern on its sides. It differs from most small orbweavers in that the distal end of the abdomen has two points. Females are 6 to 9 mm long; males are 5 to 6.5 mm.

Web & Hunting Technique: The orb web is one of the most remarkable made by any spider. The "basilica" of the Basilica Orbweaver is actually an orb web that has been pulled upward by a complex network of silk suspension threads and stretched into a dome. The female sits upside down in the middle of the dome.

Egg Sac & Eggs: The egg sacs, rough-edged, gray spheroids, are suspended above the Basilica's dome on a very tough silk line in chains of up to ten sacs.

Range: Potomac River south to Florida west to Colorado. Common in deciduous woods in all physiographic provinces of the Carolinas.

Nature Notes:

Very abundant along the edges of non-alluvial wetlands in the Coastal Plain of South Carolina.

The web of the Basilica Orbweaver may be confused with that of the Filmy Dome Spider (*Neriene radiata*); the Filmy Dome's web, however, does not have the orbweaver pattern of radial and spiral silk lines.

The egg sacs hang above the web.

Tuftlegged Orbweaver *Mangora placida*

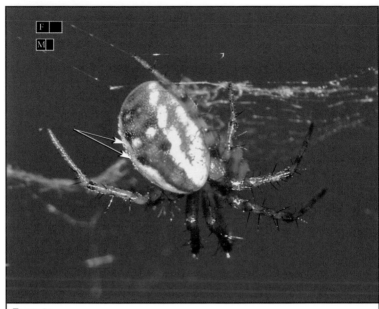

Forests.

Nature Notes:

One of the most common orbweavers in forests in early spring (Gaddy, 1981). The closely related Greenlegged Orbweaver (*Mangora maculata*) is most abundant in August and September.

This spider is creating a retreat from a folded piece of grass.

Description: The Tuftlegged Orbweaver is a small orbweaver of woodlands. It has a brownish median abdominal stripe with diagnostic pairs of white and black spots ↑. The female ranges from 2.9 to 4.0 mm in length, while the male is only 2.3 to 2.5 mm long.

Web & Hunting Technique: A small orbweb is built about one meter to one and one-half meters off of the ground.

Life Cycle: The Tuftlegged Orbweaver matures earlier than the other two common species of *Mangora*. In the Coastal Plain of South Carolina, this spider was frequently seen in March (Gaddy, 1981), and in the Mountains, it was common in April and May. It appears to mature about the same time as the Orchard Orbweaver (*Leucage venusta*).

Range: Eastern United States. Common throughout the Carolinas.

Lined Orbweaver *Mangora gibberosa*

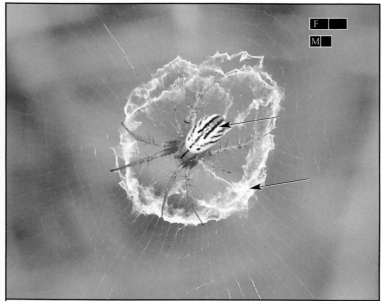

F ▮
M ▮

Grassy areas and fields. Especially common in grassy pinelands and savannahs in the Coastal Plain.

Description: Common spiders and their webs are often conspicuous. The Lined Orbweaver's abdomen is greenish-gray with two prominent black lines ↑ on its lower portion and several black spots on the upper abdomen. The female is from 4 to 6 mm in length; the male is around 3 mm long.

Web & Hunting Technique: The Lined Orbweaver builds a low web in grasses and short shrubs. The web is distinctive in that it has as small "bulls-eye" ↑ in the middle of the orb in which the female sits.

Life Cycle: Probably overwinters as subadult as it matures in mid-summer.

Range: Eastern United States. More common in Coastal Plain of the Carolinas than in the Mountain and Piedmont Provinces.

Nature Notes:

The 'bulls-eye' in the center of the web has unknown function. But recent studies on the garden spiders (*Argiope* spp.), suggest that stabilimenta in their webs may absorb ultraviolet rays in a way that would make them attractive to insects.

The lines of the Lined Orbweaver's abdomen are quite conspicuous.

Labyrinth Orbweaver *Metepeira labyrinthea*

Forests and forest openings.

Nature Notes:

Labyrinth Orbweaver egg sacs are uniquely shaped. Note the conical top.

Description: The Labyrinth Orbweaver is identified easily by its web. The spider itself has a white butterfly pattern ↑ on the light brown to black abdomen (sometimes a double butterfly pattern). The sides of the abdomen have parallel rows of white spots. Legs banded. Females are 5.5 to 6.2 mm long; males are 4.0 to 4.5 mm.

Web & Hunting Technique: It builds a vertical orb web where it is rarely found—but adjacent and attached with silk lines—is a complex "labyrinth" of a web. Here, one finds a conical-shaped pile of debris ↑—leaves, sticks, bodies of eaten insects, etc.—under which the spider has hollowed out a retreat. If this debris pile is shaken, the female will venture out.

Egg Sac & Eggs: Its egg sacs look like small flying saucers with conical tops and bottoms.

Life Cycle: Mature in late summer/early fall.

Range: Throughout North America (west to Alaska). More common in the Appalachian Mountains and the Piedmont.

White Micrathena *Micrathena mitrata*

F
M

Forest openings in open mixed hardwoods.

Description: The White Micrathena is generally whiter than the other species of this genus and always has shorter and fewer spines. The abdomen is white with black spots and usually two dark-tipped spines. The female is 4 to 6 mm in length, while males are 3 to 5 mm.

Web & Hunting Technique: This spider makes a small (6 to 9 inches wide) tight orb-web three feet or more off the forest floor.

Life Cycle: The White Micrathena is more common in late summer and fall than are the other species of *Micrathena* in South Carolina.

Range: Eastern United States. Commonly found in the Mountain and Piedmont Provinces of the Carolinas; less common to rare in the Coastal Plain.

Nature Notes:

Gaddy (1987) found *M. mitrata* to be one of the most abundant orb-weaver in open, dry woods in the Piedmont and Mountains of South Carolina in August and September. Like *Micrathena gracilis*, it is usually found in open mixed hardwoods.

Abdomen undersides are also boldly marked.

Spined Micrathena *Micrathena gracilis*

F	
M	

Forests and forest openings.

Nature Notes:

The female is quite conspicuous with her pairs of spines. Because of this species' long and abundant spines, it appears to have no predators.

Like the Spinybacked Orbweaver, it may be handled by its spines with no danger to the handler.

Males of this species are seen more frequently than the males of any of the other species of *Micrathena* or *Gasteracantha*.

Description: The Spined Micrathena is also sometimes called the Crab Spider and is, as its name indicates, shaped like a crab with protruding paired spines scattered along its elliptically-shaped abdomen. The abdomen is generally black or brown and white with four to five pairs of black-tipped spines. The female is 7.5 to 10 mm in length, while the male is up to 5 mm.

Web & Hunting Technique: The web is built about head-high to one meter off the forest floor. The female sits head up in the middle of the orb web (25 to 30 cm in diameter) day and night.

Egg Sac & Eggs: The eggs sacs, rarely seen, are constructed in autumn.

Life Cycle: The Spined Micrathena is one of the most abundant orbweavers in the Carolinas in open mixed hardwoods in early to mid-summer.

It is no wonder how this spider got its common name. The abdomen is covered in spines.

Range: Eastern United States east of the Rockies. Abundant in the Carolinas.

Viewed from the side, the unique shape of the spider becomes visible.

The much smaller male (below) approaches the larger female.

Arrowshaped Micrathena *Micrathena sagittata*

Forests, shrubby thickets, forest edges and openings in forests. Wet areas.

Nature Notes:

Most of the individuals I have found were in thickets in low webs and not in open woods.

It is less common in the Carolinas than both *M. gracilis* and *M. mitrata*.

This species is more common in wetlands than in uplands.

Description: The Arrowshaped Micrathena is one of the most striking orbweavers found in the Carolinas. Its shape is reminiscent of some of the neotropical spiny backs seen in the tropical rain forests of Central America and the Amazon. The abdomen is usually bright yellow with three sets of spines. The first set are found just above the cephalothorax and face upward; the second set are short and are found on the side of the abdomen; finally, the third and most conspicuous set occur on the end of the abdomen. These latter spines are several millimeters long and diverge from each other in a manner suggestive of the top of an arrowhead. The spines are usually dark brown to black on the female. The abdomen of the male does not have the final pair of long spines. The body (abdomen and cephalothorax) is 8 to 9 mm in length in females, while in males, it is 4 to 5 mm long.

This colorful Microthena is one of the most stunning orbweavers found in the Carolinas.

Web & Hunting Technique: Small to medium-sized orb web (15 to 25 cm in diameter) found one meter high and lower in woods and thickets.

Life Cycle: Unknown, but most Carolina collections of adults were in July and August. The species, therefore, appears to mature about the same time as many orbweavers.

Range: The Arrowshaped Microthena is widely scattered throughout the Carolinas but according to my experience, this species is more common in the Coastal Plain than in other physiographic provinces. Kaston (1972) gives the range as "eastern states west to Texas and Nebraska."

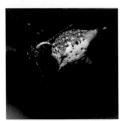

A slightly different color combination is shown here.

A close up of the stunning undersides.

Arabesque Orbweaver *Neoscona arabesca*

Non-forested areas such as fields, grasslands and shrubby sites.

Nature Notes:

Comstock (1965) said that the Arabesque Orbweaver builds webs day or night. I, however, agree with Jenkins and Howell (2004) that the species is probably nocturnal and, consequently, rarely seen in the web.

I have often collected immature females in grassy fields with a sweep net (when sweeping for jumping spiders).

This spider is one of the smallest members of the genus *Neoscona*.

Description: The Arabesque Orbweaver has an attractive but complex abdominal color pattern. On a brownish-red background, an interrupted, tapering white stripe is found. Three to four pairs of white spots with adjacent black dashes ↑ parallel the stripe on either side. The cephalothorax is brown to grayish. Legs are brown and white banded. Females are 5 to 12 mm long; males are 4 to 9 mm in length.

Web & Hunting Technique: This spider's web is usually in grasses and low shrubs and is 15 to 40 cm in diameter.

Egg Sac & Eggs: Jackman (1997) reported that its egg sac is lens-shaped and about 10 mm in diameter.

Life Cycle: Like its congeners *N. domiciliorum* and *N. crucifera*, it matures in late summer and early fall.

Note the red objects attached to the front of the abdomen. These are parasitic mites.

Range: The Arabesque Orbweaver ranges from Canada across the United States to Mexico and is more common northward. It is common, but not abundant, in all provinces of the Carolinas.

Hentz Orbweaver *Neoscona crucifera*

F

M

Found along the margins of woodlands, but most abundant around houses, warehouses and man-made structures.

Nature Notes:

Hentz Orbweaver, formerly *Neoscona hentzi*, is now called *Neoscona crucifera*.

This is primarily a nocturnal species.

Hentz Orbweaver is rarely seen in moist, dense forests, the habitat for its congener, the Spotted Forest Orbweaver (*Neoscona domiciliorum*).

Description: The abdomen is brown to rusty-brown with long conspicuous hairs. Often a faded, lighter cross can be seen in the middle of the spider's abdomen (thus, "*crucifera*"). Two to four deep, black dimples are often present near the top of the cross. The legs have brown and white bands. Females are 9 to 20 mm long; males are 5 to 15 mm in length.

Web & Hunting Technique: Its large webs are often constructed near porch lights or outside windows with indoor lamps. During the day, the spider hides on limbs or under the overhanging eaves of buildings.

Egg Sac & Eggs: The eggs are laid in a ball of wiry silk, through which they are easily visible. The egg mass—it is not a true egg "sac"—is usually attached to an overhanging limb of a tree or to the underside of the floor boards of a

The reddish femurs are quite visible on this lighter specimen. Also note the faint pale cross on the spider's abdomen.

outside porch, where rain cannot penetrate the mass.

Life Cycle: This spider appears in summer or late summer and is often present until frost.

Range: Hentz Orbweaver is found eastern North America to Canada and ranges west to the Rockies and south to Mexico. Like *Neoscona domiciliorum*, it is more common in the southern states. In the Carolinas, it is found in all physiographic provinces.

Prey is wrapped in silk for later consumption.

Spotted Forest Orbweaver *Neoscona domiciliorum*

Moist deciduous forests such as large floodplain forests, small swamp forests and moist mountain coves with waterfalls.

Nature Notes:

According to Wharton et al (1981), it was ten times more abundant than any other orb-weaver in Congaree National Park, a large, old-growth floodplain system, in South Carolina.

Males look like under-fed females (with small abdomens) and are rarely seen.

Description: A distinctively marked spider. The female's abdomen is black with a thin, white cross-like chevron on black and a row of white spots (hence the common name) along the abdomen's margins. The cephalothorax is covered with thick, long gray hairs. Femurs are bright reddish-brown, while the remaining portions of the legs are black and white banded. Females 7 to 16 mm; males 6 to 9 mm.

Web & Hunting Technique: Usually found in the center of its web day and night.

Life Cycle: Matures in mid- to late summer about the same time as is the Spined Micrathena (*Micrathena gracilis*). Some females survive until first frost.

Range: Most common in the southeast U.S., ranging north to Massachusetts. In the Carolinas, it is most abundant in the Coastal Plain, but also common in the Piedmont and Mountains.

Meadow Orbweaver *Neoscona pratensis*

F	
M	

Fields, pastures, savannahs, salt marshes, woodland edges and, of course, meadows.

Description: The Meadow Orbweaver is a small orbweaver with a reddish-brown color (the above image shows a pale specimen). The dorsum of the abdomen is lined with alternating brown, black and reddish stripes. All legs have long, widely-spaced black spines. Females are around 10 mm long; males are approximately 8 mm.

Web & Hunting Technique: The Meadow Orbweaver builds a low, small (and rarely seen) orb in which it catches its prey.

Life Cycle: Young hatch in the late summer and fall and overwinter as spiderlings or subadults.

Range: More common in the Coastal Plain, but found throughout the Carolinas. Eastern United States west to North Dakota and Louisiana.

Nature Notes:

A spider often caught in sweep nets in fields.

The Meadow Orbweaver does not resemble other *Neoscona*, but recent taxonomic research has placed it in this genus.

Other names include *Araneus pratensis* and *Singa pratensis*.

Triangulate Orbweaver *Verrucosa arenata*

Prefers dense, moist hardwoods (floodplain and cove forests). Occasionally seen in dry, open hardwood Piedmont forests

Nature Notes:

The male of this species, with its long front legs and large spines, is one of the most spectacular of the orbweavers.

Description: The Triangulate Orbweaver has a distinctive yellow to white triangle ↑ (often pink on males) shaped like an arrowhead covering the dorsum of its abdomen. The remainder of the spider's body is brownish to reddish with black markings. The female is approximately 9 mm in length; the male is usually around 6 mm long. Leg I and Leg II in males are much longer than those of females, and Leg II has a prominent, long spine on its tibia (see excellent illustration drawn by Emerton, 1903).

Web & Hunting Technique: The Triangulate Orbweaver sits in its web with its head point upward, somewhat unusual in orbweavers. According to Levi (1976) the Triangulate Orbweaver's web is made at night or in the early morning hours and is taken down at sunrise. Gaddy and Morse (1985), however, point out that in shady floodplain

The triangle of the adults can be yellow (as on left) or white (right individual) or pink (as in some males). Because of the triangle it is sometimes called the Arrowhead Spider.

woods in dark Mountain coves, Triangulate Orbweavers often sit in the web all day.

Life Cycle: The Triangulate Orbweaver matures late in the summer to early fall, usually being found about the same time as the White Micrathena (*Micrathena mitrata*).

Range: The Triangulate Orbweaver is found from Long Island south to Florida and west to Nebraska and California, according to Kaston (1978). In the Carolinas, this spider is much more common in the Mountains and Piedmont than in the Coastal Plain.

Wolf Spiders
Family Lycosidae

Description
The wolf spiders are hunting ground spiders usually brown, gray or black in color. They are medium to large spiders, ranging from 5 to 30 mm in body length. They have eight eyes in three rows (four, two and two). They have long legs and can move very quickly.

Similar Spiders
The fishing or nursery web spiders (pisaurids) are very similar to the wolf spiders, but they have smaller eyes and are usually found near water. Some grass spiders of the Agelenidae look like wolf spiders, but they have long spinnerets that protrude from under the abdomen and build sheet webs with funnel retreats.

Habitat
Forests, meadows, savannahs, beaches and rocky areas; rarely seen in houses and outbuildings.

Hunting Techniques/Web
Wolf spiders do not build webs or retreats. They hunt on the ground throughout their lives.

Eggs Sacs and Eggs
The female attaches the egg sac to the rear of her abdomen near the spinnerets where it is carried until the spiderlings hatch. After hatching, they climb onto the female's abdomen and live there until they are old enough to leave and hunt on their own.

Observations
In habitats such as rich woods and high floodplains, thousands of immature wolf spiders can be found in the leaf litter in the spring and early summer.

Diversity (Species Richness/Range)
There are approximately 300 species of lycosid spiders found in North America. According to Gaddy and Morse (1985) and Coyle (2008), there are probably around 30 species of wolf spiders that occur in the Carolinas.

Wolf Spiders (Family Lycosidae)

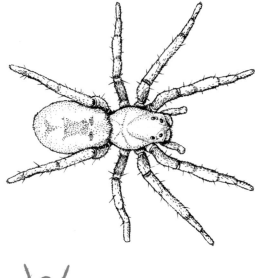

**Actual size of adult female
Beach Wolf Spider**

face

Beach Wolf Spider *Arctosa littoralis*

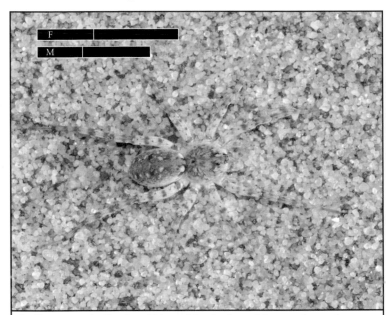

As its name indicates, this spider is found in sandy environments—beaches, sand bars and sand dunes.

Nature Notes:

Howell and Jenkins (2004) report that this species has blue-green eyeshine that can be spotted at night through the use of a headlamp or flashlight.

Its colors camouflage it well in sandy environments where it often hides.

Extremely fast runner; may even hop when alarmed.

Description: The Beach or Sand Wolf Spider is mottled with gray, white and beige all over its body and legs. Males and females range from 11 to 15 mm in length.

Web & Hunting Technique: Like other wolf spiders, the Beach Wolf is a hunter and does not build webs. This spider is often most active at night.

Egg Sac & Eggs: The female carries the large egg sac attached to its spinnerets or in its fangs until the spiderlings hatch. The spiderlings crawl on the female's abdomen and "ride" the mother until they are large enough to hunt and fend for themselves.

Life Cycle: Young hatch in the late summer and fall and overwinter as spiderlings or subadults. According to Kaston (1981), some wolf spiders may be double brooded (producing two egg sacs per year).

The Beach Wolf Spider is at home on sandy substrates. Its coloration matches the sand grains in size, shape and color!

Range: The Beach Wolf Spider is found throughout the United States wherever sandy habitats are available.

Carolina Wolf Spider *Hogna carolinensis*

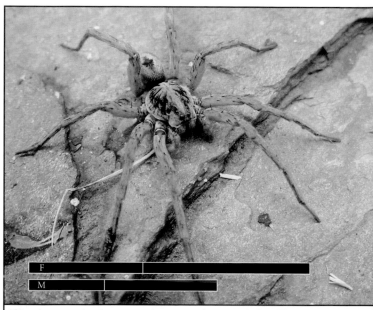

F

M

Woods, wood edges, pastures and around dwellings.

Nature Notes:

The Carolina Wolf Spider often makes its own burrow in which it hides during daylight hours.

At night in fields and grassy areas, a strong flashlight will illuminate the eyes of the Carolina Wolf Spider.

The Carolina Wolf Spider was proclaimed "State Spider of South Carolina" by the state legislature in 2000.

Description: The Carolina Wolf Spider is one of the largest hunting spiders in the state. It is rivaled only by the fishing spiders (*Dolomedes* spp.) in size. The females are darker, usually grey and black, with a narrow brown stripe on the cephalothorax. The males are brown and grey with black markings on the abdomen and a brown stripe on a black background on the cephalothorax. In both sexes, the underside (venter) of the abdomen and the cephalothorax is black. Females are 22 to 35 mm in length; males are 18 to 22 mm.

Web & Hunting Technique: The Carolina Wolf Spider is a hunter and does not build a web. It is generally nocturnal but is occasionally seen in the daytime. Like most large hunting spiders, the Carolina Wolf Spider is very quick and will attack the moving human hand.

Egg Sac & Eggs: The female carries the large egg sac in its fangs until the spiderlings

The Carolina Wolf Spider is a huge spider. The only other spiders that rival it in size would be the fishing spiders (*Dolomedes* spp.) and the Golden Silk Orbweaver (*Nephila clavipes*).

hatch. They then crawl on the female's abdomen and "ride" the mother until they are large enough to hunt and fend for themselves. From a distance, the young on the abdomen of the female wolf spider gives the appearance that the female is extremely hairy.

This is a darker individual than most.

Life Cycle: Young hatch in the late summer and fall and overwinter as spiderlings or subadults.

Range: Locally common in the Carolinas. Found throughout North America.

Stone Thinlegged Wolf Spider *Pardosa lapidicina*

F
M

Rock piles, cliffs, flatrocks, rocky areas along streams and rivers.

Nature Notes:

Grayish-green Stone Thinlegged Wolf Spiders with light mottling were found to be common on a granitic flatrock in Pickens County, South Carolina (Kelley, 1979). Their coloration matched the rock substrate.

These spiders are well-camouflaged and are often motionless when alarmed. When forced to flee, they are extremely fast.

Description: One of the so-called "thin-legged" wolf spiders. It is mottled black, brown, gray, greenish and yellow in color. The alternating light and dark bands ↑ on all eight legs are distinctive. It has light spots on the dorsum of its abdomen. The female is 7.7 to 9.3 mm long; males are 6 to 7 mm in length.

Web & Hunting Technique: Pursue prey over rocky ground.

Egg Sac & Eggs: The female carries the large egg sac attached to its spinnerets or in its fangs until the spiderlings hatch. The spiderlings crawl on the female's abdomen and "ride" the mother until they are large enough to hunt and fend for themselves.

Life Cycle: Young hatch in the late summer and fall and overwinter as spiderlings or subadults.

Range: This spider is known from New England south to Alabama and west to the Texas and Nebraska.

Shore Thinlegged Wolf Spider *Pardosa milvina*

F

M

Fields, dry woods, lake and pond margins on sand or mud.

Description: Another of the "thin-legged" wolf spiders. It is mottled black, brown, and yellow in color. A yellowish-brown stripe down the dorsum of the spider's cephalothorax meets a series of paired black-brown spots and/or chevrons ↑ on the abdomen. The female is 5.2 to 6.2 mm long; males are 4 to 4.7 mm.

Web & Hunting Technique: Wolf spiders hunt without webs.

Egg Sac & Eggs: The female carries the large egg sac attached to its spinnerets or in its fangs until the spiderlings hatch.

Life Cycle: Young hatch in the late summer and fall and overwinter as spiderlings or subadults. Howell and Jenkins (2004) indicate that *Pardosa milvina* is double brooded (producing two egg sacs per year) in the South.

Range: This spider is known from New England south to Florida and west to the Rockies.

Nature Notes:

This species is known to hop across the ground when alarmed and may be locally abundant.

In a two-year study of tilled and untilled fields in the Coastal Plain of South Carolina, 225 *Pardosa milvina* individuals were caught in pitfall traps (Gaddy and Morse, 1985).

Rabid Wolf Spider *Rabidosa rabida*

F

M

Common in woods and non-forested areas.

Nature Notes:

A close cousin, the Dotted Wolf Spider (*Rabidosa punctulata*) is very similar but the dark stripe on the dorsum of the abdomen is unbroken (no light spots) and there are black spots on the underside of the abdomen.

Note the light spots that break up the dark abdomen stripe.

Description: Light brown with dark brown stripes. Dark stripe down abdomen is broken by light angled spots near posterior ↑. Females 16 to 21 mm in length; males 11 to 12 mm.

Web & Hunting Technique: Wolf spiders are hunters and usually do not build webs. They chase down prey like wolves, hence the common name.

Egg Sac & Eggs: The female carries the large egg sac attached to its spinnerets until the spiderlings hatch. The spiderlings ↑ crawl on the female's abdomen and "ride" the mother until they are large enough to hunt and fend for themselves (see main photo this page).

Life Cycle: Young hatch in the late summer and fall and overwinter as spiderlings or subadults.

Range: Found from New England to Florida and west to Oklahoma and Nebraska.

Lance **Wolf Spider** *Schizocosa avida*

F	
M	

Open fields, pastures, around residences and in woodlands.

Description: The Lance Wolf Spider is brownish is color and has a distinctive V-shaped pattern ↑ on the dorsum of the abdomen. The inner portion of the V is nearly black, while the outer portion is light brown. The V itself is beige to yellow and points down toward the spider's spinnerets. The female is 10 to 15mm long; males are 8 to 11 mm.

Web & Hunting Technique: No web. Hunt prey by pursuit.

Egg Sac & Eggs: The female carries the large egg sac attached to her spinnerets or in her fangs until the spiderlings hatch.

Life Cycle: Young appear in late summer and overwinter in the leaf litter or ground layer where thousands may be seen on warm winter days. Adulthood is reached in May or June.

Range: Most Carolina records are from the Mountains and Piedmont provinces. Ranges throughout the United States and Canada.

Nature Notes:

After hatching, the spiderlings crawl on the female's abdomen and get a free ride on mom's abdomen until they are large enough to hunt and fend for themselves.

Nursery web or Fishing Spiders Family Pisauridae

Description

The nursery web or fishing spider species are extremely large, long-legged spiders found near water. The overall length (body and legs) of the Dark Fishing Spider (*Dolomedes tenebrosus*) is equaled only by the Golden Silk Orbweaver (*Nephila clavipes*) and the Carolina Wolf Spider (*Hogna carolinensis*). Females, which range from 15 to 40 mm in length, are about twice as large as males. Most of the spiders in this family are patterned with gray, white and brown colors.

Similar Spiders

The fishing spiders are often mistakenly called wolf spiders. The true wolf spiders of the family Lycosidae, however, have extremely large posterior median eyes and are not common in and around water.

Habitat

Forests, marshes, and openings near bodies of water. *Dolomedes tenebrosus* has been found considerably upslope from bodies of water in mixed deciduous woods.

Hunting Techniques/Web

Most of the fishing spiders hunt for prey near or in water. They have been known to dive for several minutes and catch small minnows (they hold air bubbles in the hairs on their legs). [The "Diving Bell" Spider of Europe (*Argyroneta aquatica*), which keeps a large bubble of air in an underwater web, is in the Family Cybaeidae.]

Eggs Sacs and Eggs

A large spherical egg sac is carried in the jaws of the female in spiders of the genus *Dolomedes*. In *Pisaurina*, the nursery web spiders, the female folds over a leave and makes an egg sac. She waits there until the spiderlings hatch out.

Diversity (Species Richness/Range)

There about 15 species of fishing spiders in North America (Carico, 1973). In the Carolinas, there are seven known species (Gaddy and Morse, 1985).

Nursery Web or Fishing Spiders (Family Pisauridae)

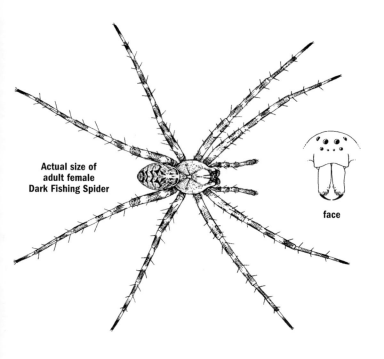

**Actual size of
adult female
Dark Fishing Spider**

face

White Fishing Spider *Dolomedes albineus*

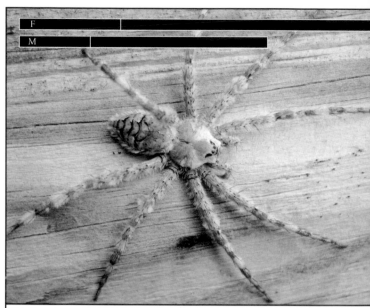

F

M

Wetlands and near bodies of water; often found on tree trunks.

Nature Notes:

Carico (1973) notes that *D. albineus* is found higher up in trees while *D. tenebrosus*, which also occurs in southern swamps, is usually found within a few feet of the water line.

Carico (1973) stated that it has been found congregating in large numbers in tree hollows and crevices in Florida, perhaps in a "mating swarm," a type of behavior rare in spiders.

Occasionally found as far north as Great Smoky Mountains National Park.

Description: A very large grayish-white spider. It, as its name indicates, is much lighter than *D. tenebrosus*, especially the dorsum of the cephalothorax. Females are 23 to 30 mm long; males are 18 to 20 mm.

Web & Hunting Technique: A sit-and-wait predator that camouflages itself on gray bark or gray-white rocks along bodies of water and pounces on passing prey.

Egg Sac & Eggs: The female produces an egg sac that she carries in her chelicerae (fangs) until the young hatch. It then makes a nursery web amongst leaves and guards it until her death.

Life Cycle: Matures in July when it is frequently seen at night, often ranging a considerable distance from water.

Range: Much more common in the Coastal Plain but sporadically seen in the Blue Ridge . Ranges from Florida to the Appalachians of North Carolina and up the Mississippi basin to central Kentucky and southern Missouri (Carico, 1973).

Whitewater Fishing Spider *Dolomedes scriptus*

Fast-flowing, oxygenated "whitewater" rivers and streams.

Description: White Ws on abdomen. Lighter around edges of abdomen and cephalothorax. Females 18 to 30 mm; males 12 to 18 mm. Males have longer legs than females and can have a 85 mm legspan.

Web & Hunting Technique: Dives beneath the surface of the water, carrying bubbles of air on the hairs of its legs as it goes down. Feeds primarily on invertebrates, but small minnows and other immature fish are occasionally caught.

Egg Sac & Eggs: Egg sacs carried by the female to nurseries in low vegetation along rivers and streams. Nursery webs and eggs sacs are rarely seen.

Life Cycle: Common in summer months along mountain rivers and streams. Males seek females in early to mid-August for mating and can often been seen stalking her on river rocks.

Range: Found north to Canada, south to Florida and west to Nebraska. In the Carolinas, primarily in the Mountain Province.

Nature Notes:

The Whitewater Fishing Spider perches on logs and rocks in streams and dives into the cold, clear water in search of prey.

As its name indicates, this spider is a denizen of fast-moving rocky streams and rivers. Unlike its closely-related congener, *Dolomedes vittatus,* it prefers open, sunny areas in rivers and streams. [*D. vittatus* is found in small, shaded streams (Carico, 1973).]

Dark Fishing Spider *Dolomedes tenebrosus*

Wetlands. Commonly found on tree trunks, but, in late summer, often seen in houses, outbuildings, and around porch lights.

Nature Notes:

Often mistakenly called a "wolf spider."

The Dark Fishing Spider wanders farther away from water than any of the fishing spiders and often mates and lays eggs a good distance from wetland habitats.

During the day, the spider hides out in stumps and holes in tree trunks. On cloudy days, the Dark Fishing Spider is often seen in swamps camouflaged on grey hardwood trunks.

Description: One of the largest spiders in North America—equaled or surpassed in size only by the Golden Silk Orbweaver (*Nephila clavipes*) and the Carolina Wolf Spider (*Hogna carolinensis*)—the Dark Fishing Spider is from 15 to 40 mm in length (females). Its long legs, with alternating dark and light stripes and black spines, often reach 100 mm in length. Dark, masklike face ↑. It has four dark Ws on its abdomen ↑ and closely resembles *Dolomedes albineus*, which is usually lighter and occurs in the swamps and large wetlands of the Coastal Plain. *Dolomedes tenebrosus* is most closely related taxonomically to *Dolomedes okefinokeensis*, which is rare and known only from southern Georgia and Florida.

Web & Hunting Technique: The Dark Fishing Spider sits and waits for passing crawling or flying insects, which it catches with ease. Being a hunter, this spider is somewhat

This Dark Fishing Spider has shed its skin and is about to leave it behind. The spiders are very vulnerable to predators at this time.

aggressive and extremely quick. It will dive at and attack any moving object, including the human hand.

Egg Sac & Eggs: The female produces a spherical egg sac and, like most species in this genus, carries it in its chelicerae (fangs) until the young hatch. It then makes a nursery web amongst leaves and guards it until her death.

Life Cycle: In the Carolinas, the Dark Fishing Spider matures in July when it is frequently seen a night.

Range: Ranges northeast to Newfoundland, northwest to Manitoba, west to Texas and Nebraska and south to the panhandle of Florida. It is found throughout the Carolinas.

Tree cavities, outhouses, homes—all used as shelter.

A face only a mother could love!

The shed skin of the head and cephalothorax.

Sixspotted Fishing Spider *Dolomedes triton*

Rarely seen away from ponds and lakes.

Nature Notes:

The Sixspotted Fishing Spider is often seen on a water lily (*Nymphaea odorata*) pad with a minnow or small fish in its fangs.

While reviewing the spider collection of the Charleston Museum, I found a specimen of this species collected in the 1930s (probably with a dip net) from the Edisto River along the coast of South Carolina. After careful examination, I saw that the spider still had a fish about 5 mm in length in its fangs.

(continued on next page)

Description: The Sixspotted Fishing Spider is so named not because of the parallel white spots on the back of its abdomen ↑ (which usually number over six), but because of six spots on its venter or underside. This is a beautiful spider, mostly black and white in color, with two white lines along the margins of its abdomen. It is generally found walking on water or on aquatic vegetation in ponds and lakes. Female is 17 to 20mm long; male is 9 to 13mm.

Web & Hunting Technique: This spider, like other fishing spiders, does actually dive beneath the surface of the water. It carries bubbles of air on the hairs of its legs as it goes down. It generally catches invertebrates, but small minnows and other immature fish species are occasionally caught.

Egg Sac & Eggs: Carried by female in fangs. Placed in nurseries in marshes later in the year.

Unlike its *Dolomedes* cousins, the Sixspotted Fishing Spider rarely wanders far from its aquatic home. It is also quite a bit smaller in size.

Life Cycle: Carico (1973) noted that the Sixspotted Fishing Spider was found year-round in southern climates. In South Carolina, it can be seen almost any month of the year on barrier islands and in the Outer Coastal Plain. In the Mountains, spiderlings hatch out in the fall and overwinter as subadults.

Range: Like *Dolomedes tenebrosus, D. triton* is a wide-ranging species. It is known from Chiapas, Mexico to Hudson Bay in Canada and west to California and north to the Alaskan border. It is common throughout the Carolinas.

(Nature Notes continued)

Like water striders (insects of the Order Hemiptera, the Family Gerridae), which are sometimes mistakenly called "waters spiders," its legs are covered with small hairs that elevate it slightly and allow it to glide over the surface of the water. Where the spider rests, small dimples appear in the water's surface tension.

Nursery Web Spider *Pisaurina mira*

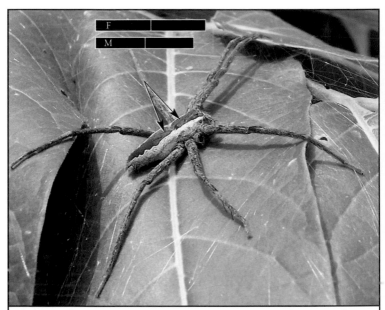

Margins of wetlands, particularly non-forested wetlands such as marshes. Also moist meadows, old fields and wet pine savannah.

Nature Notes:

The female Nursery Web Spider usually selects a low herbaceous or graminaceous plant with broad leaves and folds the upper leaf over after laying the egg sac. The web is then built around the folded leaf and the egg sac.

I once observed a Nursery Web Spider with spiderlings under the hood of the pitchers of an insectivorous pitcher-plant (*Sarracenia flava*) in a wet pine savannah.

Description: The Nursery Web Spider is a large spider that has a body reminiscent of a wolf spider with fishing spider legs. It is generally light brown with a broad, white-margined dark brown band ↑ down the middle of the abdomen continuing onto the carapace of the cephalothorax. Females are 12 to 16 mm in length, while males are about 10 to 15 mm.

Web & Hunting Technique: Like other members of this family, the Nursery Web Spider hunts near water, but does not walk on the water's surface or dive for prey.

Egg Sac & Eggs: A web is not built for hunting or resting; however, in late summer and fall after mating, the female lays an oval egg sac and constructs a dense, amorphous web around the egg sac (see photo next page). The female then stays with the egg sac until after the spiderlings hatch and disperse, usually late in autumn.

The white-edged dark stripe that continues from the carapace onto the abdomen is diagnostic in this species. This one is eating a fly.

Life Cycle: Appears to overwinter as spiderlings or subadults. Matures in late summer.

Range: This spider is found throughout the Carolinas. It is known from New England south to Florida, west to Nebraska.

The female makes a shapeless web around the egg sac that will serve as the nursery for the spiderlings.

Lynx Spiders
Family Oxyopidae

Description

The lynx spiders are medium-sized spiders ranging from about 5 to 10 mm in length. They can be recognized by three distinctive features: 1) their legs are unusually spiny; 2) their abdomens taper to a point just above the spinnerets; and 3) their eyes have a unique arching pattern.

carapace

face

Similar Spiders

None.

Habitat

On tall grasses, flower heads, in shrubs.

Hunting Techniques/Web

The lynxes are notorious daytime predators. They have excellent vision, although their eyes are slightly smaller than those of the jumping spiders, and they are quick. They do not build webs, but, instead, sit and wait (usually camouflaged) for prey.

Eggs Sacs and Eggs

The eggs sacs of lynx spiders are brownish with a consistency of paper and are somewhat amorphous in shape. The female guards the egg case until the spiderlings hatch—normally in autumn.

Diversity (Species Richness/Range)

There are around 20 species of this family in North America. In the Carolinas, fewer than five species are known. (Gaddy & Morse, 1985).

Lynx Spiders (Family Oxyopidae)

Actual size of adult female Striped Lynx Spider

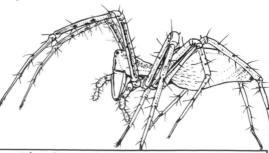

Striped Lynx Spider *Oxyopes salticus*

F

M

♀

Found primarily in grassy fields.

Description: The lynx spiders are very distinctive. Eyes are clustered on a prominent cephalothoracic mound, long spines (usually black) on the legs and tapered abdomens. It is yellowish-brown with various longitudinal stripes on the cephalothorax and the abdomen. A small diamond pattern ↑ is often found on female's abdomen; the abdomen of the male is frequently iridescent. Females are 5.7 to 6.7 mm in length; males are 4 to 4.5 mm.

Web & Hunting Technique: Brady (1964) noted that "...this spider postures itself in grasses and on herbs like a crab spider, but jumps and leaps about with greater energy than jumping spiders."

Egg Sac & Eggs: Eggs are laid on grasses and herbs and are guarded by the female until frost.

Life Cycle: Overwinters as immatures and matures in June to July.

Range: Ranges throughout the United States.

Nature Notes:

Found in nearly every county in North and South Carolina.

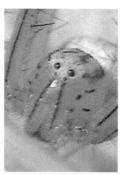

The high mounded cephalothorax is evident in this front view.

Green Lynx Spider *Peucetia viridans*

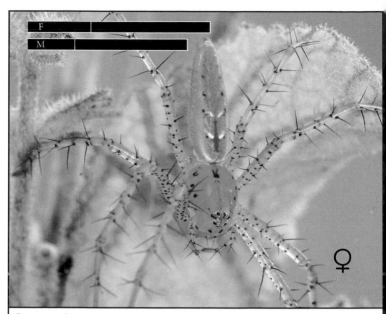

F

M

♀

Savannahs, grassy roadsides, flower gardens and meadows.

Nature Notes:

Green Lynx often fills the ecological niche of the crab spiders of the families Thomisidae and Philodromidae in the South. Farther north where the Green Lynx is absent, crab spiders are much more abundant.

♂

Males have thinner abdomens and are smaller.

Description: The Green Lynx cannot be mistake for any other spider. In the summer, it has a bright green body and red spots with paler green legs covered with long black spines. In fall, the surviving females often turn light brown for camouflage on the brown egg sacs, but they still have reddish spots and long, numerous black spines on the legs. Females are from 14 to 16 mm long; males have thinner abdomens and are 12 to 13 mm long and have much longer legs.

Web & Hunting Technique: The Green Lynx is a "sit-and-wait" predator that spends most of its lifetime on or near flowers, where it camouflages itself amongst leaves and on floral sepals or bracts. When insects land on the flowers in search of nectar, they pounce (thus, their name) and quickly bite the back of the head at the base of its nerve ganglia. It is common to see an immobile bumble bee on a bright flower, only to discover that it is being

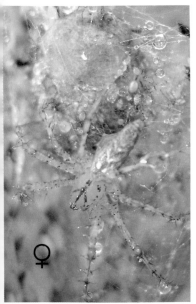

♀

A female guards her egg sac.

They can change color somewhat to match the plant they are hunting on.

held and eaten by a Green Lynx. In addition to bees, flies and wasps, they also capture moths, butterflies and even dragonflies. In the fall, I have even seen migrating Monarch butterflies captured by the Green Lynx.

Green Lynxes can even take down a Monarch!

Egg Sac & Eggs: Late in the summer, the female deposits a brownish, irregularly-shaped egg sac on vegetation and tenaciously guards it until she dies (see image above left).

Life Cycle: In autumn on dewy mornings, the brown female can often be found with hundreds of reddish-brown spiderlings, all about to disperse into the wild. The spiderlings overwinter as immatures and reach mature the following May or June.

Range: Found in the southern United States from Florida north to Virginia and west to California. In the Carolinas, the Green Lynx is abundant.

This semitranslucent spider is a real beauty.

Funnel Weavers
Family Agelenidae

Description/Similar Spiders
The funnel weavers are large (10-20 mm) spiders that make expansive sheet webs with funnel-shaped retreats. The spiders themselves are brown, black and white and look like wolf spiders. They, however, can be separated from the lycosids and other such spiders by their long (to 3 mm) protruding spinnerets.

Habitat
In grassy openings and woodlands.

Hunting Techniques/Web
Grass spiders (*Agelenopsis* species) are rarely seen outside of their web. Their webs are open, curving sheets that taper to a funnel. The spider sits at the end of the funnel, waiting for prey to land on the sheet. As soon as the prey touches the web, the spider flies out of the funnel and pounces on the prey.

Eggs Sacs and Eggs
A flat silken egg sac usually found under bark.

Diversity (Species Richness/Range)
There are around 300 species of grass spiders in North America. In the Carolinas, there are fewer than 10 species with documented occurrences (Gaddy and Morse, 1985).

Grass Spiders (Family Agelenidae)
Page 140 Grass Spider species (*Agelenopsis* spp.)

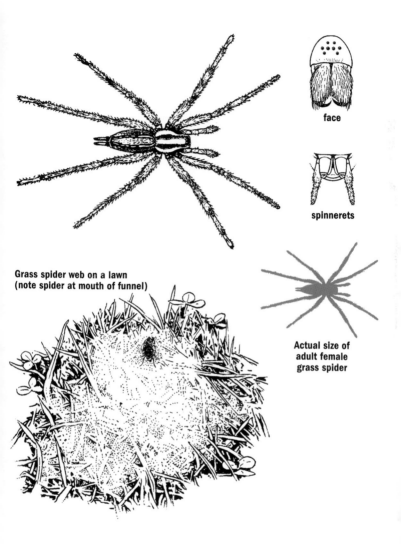

face

spinnerets

**Grass spider web on a lawn
(note spider at mouth of funnel)**

**Actual size of
adult female
grass spider**

Grass Spider species *Agelenopsis* spp.

F

M

Open woods, woods edges, shrubs, but primarily open, grassy areas. Suburban lawns.

Nature Notes:

Agelenopsis naevia is the most common grass spider species in the eastern U.S.; and probably the most common species in the Carolinas.

A little puff of breath on the web of a grass spider will bring the denizen out of the funnel expecting a meal. But this usually only works once or twice!

Description: The grass spider species (or funnel web spiders) of the genus *Agelenopsis* are difficult to separate in the field. They are rarely found outside of their distinctive web. The web is a large, curving platform that tapers into a long, funnel-shaped retreat. The spider is usually gray to brownish in color but can be pale yellow (photo right hand page). The cephalothorax has two lateral light bands and one medial light band ↑; the abdomen has two black broken light bands that may read as spotted on some individuals. This large spider could be mistaken for a wolf spider (Lycosidae) except for the long (1-2 mm), extruding spinnerets ↑. Females 16 to 20 mm long; males 13 to 18 mm.

Web & Hunting Technique: The Grass Spider's funnel webs are sometimes severa in diameter. They are most obvious after periods of drought when heavy rains ha

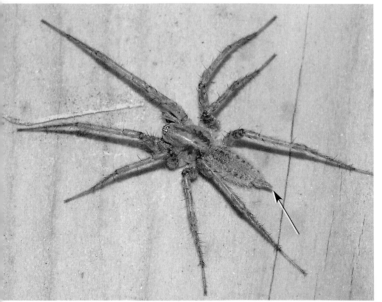

Grass spiders are often gray-black but some may be pale yellow such as this individual. Note the long spinnerets at the end of the abdomen. This trait helps separate this group from the wolf spiders of the Lycosidae.

destroyed them. The webs are not sticky. Because the spider lives in the edge of the web, it can feel the slightest vibration on the web. The spider hides in the tubular retreat until prey lands on the sheet or platform at which time the spider darts out at great speed and captures the prey (see image on left hand page). One can simulate this behavior by lightly tapping or blowing on the sheet and inducing the spider to appear.

Dozens of grass spider webs can be seen on a single lawn, especially on dewy mornings.

Egg Sac & Eggs: Flat cocoon, 8 to 9 mm long, usually found under bark (Howell and Jenkins, 2004).

Life Cycle: Matures in summer and fall; probably emerges from egg sacs in late fall or spring.

Range: *Agelenopsis naevia* is known from New England south to Florida and west to Kansas and Texas (Kaston, 1978).

Hackledmesh Weavers Family Amaurobiidae

Description/Similar Spiders

These are brown, nondescript, cribellate spiders usually 8 to 15 mm in size with a two-part cribellum. They are closely related to the Dictynidae (no species from this family are discussed in this book) and other cribellate spiders.

Similar Spiders

The Dictynidae also weave hackledmesh webs, but they are minute spiders, usually less than 4 mm in body length.

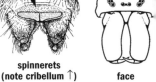

spinnerets
(note cribellum ↑)   **face**

Habitat

In woodlands under bark or rocks; on rock outcrops in openings in rock crevices. Sometimes found under and around buildings.

Hunting Techniques/Web

These spiders make interesting webs with loose, sagging or ballooning webs. There are often layers of loose sheets of silk. There is usually a small retreat for the spider.

Eggs Sacs and Eggs

No data available.

Diversity (Species Richness/Range)

There are fewer than 100 species of this family in North America. In the Carolinas, there are around twenty species known (Gaddy and Morse, 1985); (Coyle, 2008).

Hackledmesh Weavers
(Family Amaurobiidae)

Page 143 Medicine Spider (*Coras medicinalis*)

Actual size of
adult female
Medicine Spider

Medicine Spider *Coras medicinalis*

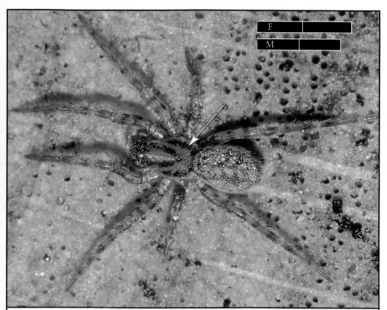

F	
M	

Under rock overhangs and loose bark, in stumps, under eaves of houses and in cellars and basements.

Description: Light brown to yellow with a complex, brown-yellow-black pattern on the cephalothorax ↑ and an abdomen slightly reminiscent of that of the Spitting Spider. The Medicine Spider, however, has shorter legs and extruding (1 to 1.5 mm) spinnerets. Females are 9 to 14 mm in length; males are 9 to 13 mm.

Web & Hunting Technique: Catches its prey in a smooth, sometimes two-layered, often curved web with a small, shallow retreat. Because of the thickness of the web, the spider usually cannot be seen. Upon close examination, however, the spider can be found and coaxed out of the web.

Life Cycle: Matures in summer and fall; probably emerges from egg sacs in late fall or spring.

Range: Throughout the Carolinas. Also known from the eastern U. S. and Canada west to Minnesota and Texas (Kaston, 1978).

Nature Notes:

I have a log cabin in the Blue Ridge of South Carolina where in late summer 25 to 50 *Coras* spiders make small webs under the basal, overhanging logs of the house.

This spider gets its name from the fact that in the distant past, a tincture derived from its web was used as a narcotic to alleviate fever (Hentz, 1821).

Sac Spiders
Family Clubionidae

Description
The clubionid family has undergone radical taxonomic changes recently. The genus *Castianiera*, which includes numerous species of ant-mimicking spiders, and several other genera of ant-mimics have been taken out of this family and placed in the Corrinidae, the antmimic spider family. Clubionids have two claws, homogeneous eyes and conical spinnerets.

Similar Spiders
The gnaphosid spiders are very similar in appearance to the clubionids; they, however, have cylindrical spinnerets. Antmimic spiders of the closely-related corrinid family are always more brightly colored.

Habitat
In leaves and under stones.

Hunting Techniques/Web
No hunting web. Hunts at night; overwinters (hibernates?) in tubular silk retreat or "sac."

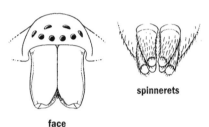

spinnerets

face

Egg Sacs and Eggs
No data available.

Diversity (Species Richness/Range)
Nearly 200 species are known from North America; approximately 15 species occur in the Carolinas (Gaddy & Morse, 1985); (Coyle, 2008).

Sac Spiders (Family Clubionidae)
Page 145 White Sac Spider (*Elaver excepta*)

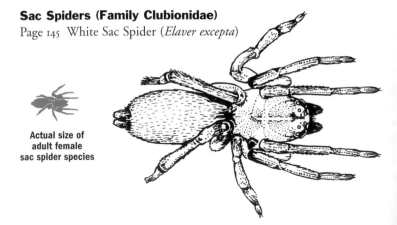

Actual size of
adult female
sac spider species

White Sac Spider *Elaver excepta (=Clubionoides e.)*

Woods in leaf litter, under stones, logs and debris.

Description: The White Sac Spider is probably the most common spider in the family
Clubionidae (the sac spiders) in South
Carolina. It has a fuzzy white abdomen with
extruding spinnerets ↑ that appear to be two
tails. The cephalothorax is clear brown, and
the legs are whitish but the femur and
metatarsus are often blackish. Females of these
spiders are from 6 to 7.5 mm in length, while
males are 4.5 to 6.5 mm long.

Web & Hunting Technique: This spider is a
hunter that does not use a web in prey capture.

Life Cycle: These spiders overwinter in dense
silky sacs. In the Coastal Plain and in on barrier islands, adults may live several years.

Range: Found throughout the Carolinas. It
ranges from New England south to Georgia
and west to Kansas and Nebraska.

Nature Notes:

The White Sac Spider is
the only clubionid spider
that appears to be
abundant in the
Carolinas. Most species
of the family are
probably overlooked.

Antmimic Spiders
Family Corrinidae

Description

Castianeira spiders, formerly in the family Clubionidae, are black- to orange spiders, most of which mimic various species of ants. Females of these spiders are from 7 to 10 mm in length, while males are 6 to 8 mm. Most move slowly and deliberately like ants.

Habitat

These ground-dwelling spiders are found in a variety of habitats from sandy shores to dry inland sand hills. They often occupy the habitat of their mimic model.

Hunting Techniques/Web

Ant mimics hunt by day. Ant mimicry is thought to be an escape from predators, but it may also be a strategy by which these spiders get closer to their prey—insects. No web is built on a daily basis, but silk is used construction the overwintering and/or protective "sac."

Egg Sacs and Eggs

The egg sacs of some *Castianeira* species are laid in crevices in rocks (or under rocks). They often have a distinctive chrome-colored outer layer (Comstock, 1940). These spiders overwinter in dense silky sacs.

Diversity (Species Richness/Range)

Gaddy and Morse (1985) list nine species of *Castianeira* from South Carolina. Coyle, (2008) lists 17 species of corrinids for the Smokies.

Corrinid Antmimic Spiders (Family Corrinidae)

Delightful Antmimic *Castianeira amoena*

Ground dwelling.

Description: A reddish-orange with dark and light bands on its abdomen and resembles red ants and female velvet ants (velvet ants are not true ants but mutillid wasps.) Females are 7 to 8.8 mm in length; males are 5.7 to 6.8 mm.

Web & Hunting Technique: No web is built on a daily basis, but silk is used construction the overwintering "sac." Ant mimicry is thought to be an escape from predators, but it may also be a strategy by which these spiders get closer to their prey—insects.

Egg Sac & Eggs: The egg sacs of some *Castianeira* species are laid in crevices in rocks (or under rocks). They often have a distinctive chrome-colored outer layer (Comstock, 1940).

Life Cycle: These spiders overwinter in dense silky sacs. In the Coastal Plain and on barrier islands, adults may live several years.

Range: This spider is generally southern in distribution, ranging from North Carolina south to Florida and west to Texas and Kansas.

Nature Notes:

Castianeira spiders were formerly in the family Clubionidae.

Gaddy and Morse (1985) listed nine species of *Castianeira* from South Carolina; there are probably more.

Coyle (2008) lists 17 species from the Smokies, four of which may be new species to science.

Twobanded Antmimic *Castianeira cingulata*

Ground dwelling.

Nature Notes:

These are ground-dwelling "sac spiders." Most move slowly and deliberately like ants.

Castianeira gertschii (Gertsch Antmimic) and *Myrmecotypus lineatus* (a genus also in the Corinnidae family) have clear, reddish bodies and look like mound-building ants in the genus *Formica*.

Description: Black to brown in ground color with two white transverse bands ↑ on the anterior portion of the dorsum of the abdomen. It is thought to be a carpenter ant (*Camponotus* spp.) mimic. Females are 6.7 to 8 mm in length; males are 6.4 to 7 mm.

Web & Hunting Technique: Ant mimicry is thought to be an escape from predators, but it may also be a strategy by which these spiders get closer to their prey—insects. No web is built on a daily basis, but silk is used construction the overwintering "sac."

Egg Sac & Eggs: The egg sacs of some *Castianeira* species are laid in crevices in rocks (or under rocks).

Life Cycle: These spiders overwinter in dense silky sacs. In the Coastal Plain and on barrier islands, adults may live several years.

Range: Reported from the Piedmont of South Carolina in Gaddy and Morse (1985), and from the Smokies of North Carolina (Coyle, 2008).

Antmimic species *Castianeira crucigera*

Ground dwelling.

Description: Hoary gray color with gray and black striped legs and distinctive black markings on its abdomen. The entire cephalothorax is a powdery gray, while the abdomen is black with a gray longitudinal band (often in the shape of a cross). The gray band invariable has a black diamond-shaped blotch ↑ in the middle of the "cross" area. Females are 6 to 8 mm in length; males are 6.5 to 6.8 mm.

Web & Hunting Technique: Ant mimicry may be a strategy by which these spiders get closer to their prey—insects. No web is built, but silk is used construction the overwintering "sac."

Egg Sac & Eggs: The egg sacs of some *Castianeira* species are laid in crevices in rocks.

Life Cycle: Overwinter in dense silky sacs. In the Coastal Plain and on barrier islands, adults may live several years.

Range: Reported from the Outer Coastal Plain of South Carolina in Gaddy and Morse (1985).

Nature Notes:

Known only from four southeastern states: South Carolina, North Carolina, Virginia and Arkansas.

Redspotted Antmimic *Castianeira descripta*

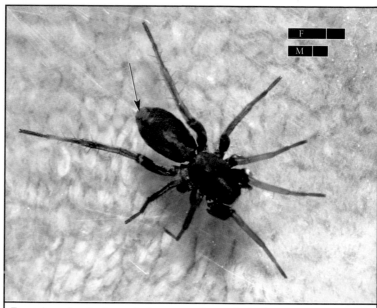

Found under logs and stones and, rarely, in houses.

Nature Notes:

Gaddy and Morse (1985) listed *Castianeira descripta* as the most common of the nine *Castianeira* species known from South Carolina.

This species may also be (see *Castianeira amoena*) a velvet ant mimic (velvet ants are not true ants but mutillid wasps).

Description: A black spider with a red to orange longitudinal stripe on the dorsum of the abdomen. The stripe often is broken into a series of reddish-orange blotches or spots ↑. Females are 8 to 10 mm in length; males are 6.2 to 7.6 mm long.

Web & Hunting Technique: Ant mimicry is thought to be an escape from predators, but it may also be a strategy by which these spiders get closer to their prey—insects. No web is built on a daily basis, but silk is used construction the overwintering "sac."

Egg Sac & Eggs: The egg sacs of some *Castianeira* species are laid in crevices in rocks.

Life Cycle: These spiders overwinter in dense silky sacs. In the Coastal Plain and on barrier islands, adults may live several years.

Range: More common in the Coastal Plain than farther inland. Found from southern Canada throughout the United States west to the Rockies.

Carpenter Antmimic *Castianeira longipalpus*

Found under logs and stones and, rarely, in houses.

Description: A black spider with transverse white bands ↑ on its abdomen and Legs III and IV (the back legs). The cephalothorax is black mottled with white dots. It is also a carpenter ant (*Camponotus* spp.) mimic. Females are 7 to 10 mm in length; males are 5.5 to 6.1 mm.

Web & Hunting Technique: No web is built on a daily basis, but silk is used construction the overwintering "sac."

Egg Sac & Eggs: The egg sacs of some *Castianeira* species are laid in crevices in rocks.

Life Cycle: These spiders overwinter in dense silky sacs. In the Coastal Plain and on barrier islands, adults may live several years.

Range: It has been reported from the Mountains to the Coastal Plain (Gaddy and Morse, 1985); (Coyle, 2008). This species ranges from southern Canada and New England west to the Pacific Northwest and in the southeastern United States west to Oklahoma.

Nature Notes:

Howell and Jenkins (2004) notes that *C. longipalpus* raises its forelegs to mimic the antennae of carpenter ants. This spider is often found in carpenter ant colonies.

Most antmimics move slowly and deliberately like ants.

Stealthy Ground Spiders
Family Gnaphosidae

Spiders of the gnaphosid ground spiders have two rows of four eyes. They live under bark and stones and are generally nocturnal. There are over 200 species known in North America. In South Carolina, about 25 gnaphosid ground spiders have been collected (Gaddy and Morse, 1985). Of this family, only the Parson Spider (*Herpyllus ecclesiasticus*) is common in the Carolinas.

Stealthy Ground Spiders (Family Gnaphosidae)

face

spinnerets

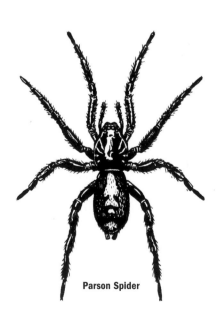

Parson Spider

**Actual size of
adult female
Parson Spider**

Twolined Cesonia *Cesonia bilineata*

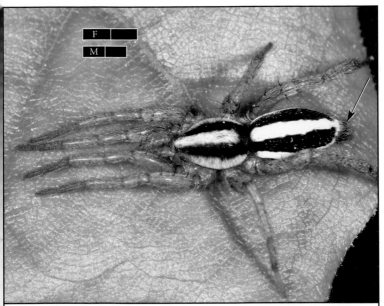

Under rocks and leaf litter in woods, rarely entering houses.

Description: This gnaphosid (family Gnaphosidac) spider roughly resembles a small grass or funnel web spider (family Agelenidae). There are two black stripes that extend from the cephalothorax to the end of the abdomen with a whitish line separating them. The spinnerets in this species are obvious and often protrude from the abdomen 1 mm or so ↑. Females are 6 to 8 mm in length, while males are 5 to 6 mm.

Web & Hunting Technique: They hunt primarily at night on the ground. They often appear on the top of the leaf litter after heavy rains. Most gnaphosids have a silken tubular retreat under leaves or stones.

Life Cycle: In the Piedmont and Mountains, they probably hibernate in sacs. Along the coast, they overwinter in leaf litter or in grassy areas.

Range: Sporadic through the Carolinas; probably overlooked. It ranges from New England to Georgia and west to Nebraska.

Nature Notes:

This spider resembles grass spiders of the genus *Agelenopsis*, but is much smaller.

Parson Spider *Herpyllus ecclesiasticus*

Woods, under logs, near houses, under boards and in houses, churches and other dwellings.

Nature Notes:

The common name may come from the abdomen markings resembling the white clerical collar of a parson.

There have been Parson Spiders in every house in which I have ever lived.

It is a quick spider with erratic movements and is very difficult to catch or to photograph.

See Majeski and Durst (1975b) for comments on the bite of this spider.

Description: A small black spider with a unique white mark including a bold white chevron ↑ on its abdomen and what appears to be a forked tail. The "tail" is an extension of the spinnerets (curiously not visible in the photo). Females are 8 to 13 mm long; males are 5 to 7 mm.

Web & Hunting Technique: Hunts in debris and in the leaf litter of the forest floor. In dwellings, it probably eats small insects (including baby roaches). Silk is used in the construction of an overwintering or "hibernation" sac; no web is built to capture prey.

Egg Sac & Eggs: Makes a flat egg sac under tree bark and wood in the fall.

Life Cycle: Active year round in dwellings. It probably overwinters in the spiderling or subadult stage in the woods.

Range: Common throughout the Carolinas. Known from New England south to Georgia and west to Oklahoma and Colorado.

Hooded Sergiolus Antmimic *Sergiolus capulatus*

F
M

Found in leaf litter. Often appear on top of leaf litter after rains.

Description: This beautiful little spider is probably a mutillid wasp ("velvet ant") mimic. *Sergiolus* spiders are brightly marked with orange, black and white patterns. Females are around 10 mm in length, while males are 5.5 to 7 mm.

Web & Hunting Technique: Hunt in the leaf litter of forests. Ant mimicry is thought to be an escape from predators, but may also help these spiders get closer to their prey—insects. Silk is used in the construction of an overwintering or "hibernation" sac; no web is built to capture prey.

Life Cycle: Along the coast, these spiders probably overwinter in leaf litter or in grassy areas. In the Piedmont and Mountains, they probably hibernate in sacs.

Range: Sporadic through the Carolinas; probably overlooked. Species of *Sergiolus* are found from New England south to Florida and west to Texas, Oklahoma and Nebraska.

Nature Notes:

There are at least five species of *Sergiolus* known from South Carolina (Gaddy and Morse, 1985) and three whose ranges overlap the state.

Howell and Jenkins (2004) found *Sergiolus capulatus* living in groups with its own species and other "look-alike" *Sergiolus* species. No detailed studies on the dynamics of ant mimicry in this species are known.

Running Crab Spiders
Family Philodromidae

Description
The running crab spiders are similar in body shape to the true crab spiders (thomisids); however, they lack the bright coloration seen in the family Thomisidae. Most philodromids are dull brown or gray. They also are generally larger than the thomisids, ranging from 7 to 15 mm in size. The primary diagnostic feature that separates the two families is the fact that Leg II is longer than Leg I in the philodromids. In *Ebo latithorax*, one of the smallest running crab spiders, Leg II is grossly longer than Leg I.

Similar Spiders
The thomisids or true crab spiders are similar to the running crab spiders, but the thomisids are brighter, generally associated with flowers and are smaller than the philodromids.

Habitat
In fields, savannahs, meadows and woodlands. The running crab spiders are more likely to be found in woodlands than the true crab spiders.

Hunting Techniques/Web
The philodromids hunt both by chasing prey and by sitting in wait for prey while camouflaged.

Eggs and Egg Sac
The bright-white egg sac is attached to twigs or bark, oftentimes in the fork between a branch and the main stem of the shrub or tree (see illustration in Comstock, 1965).

Observations
Unlike most spiders, the running crab spiders overwinter as subadults and lay their eggs in spring and early summer. (The widows, *Latrodectus* spp. in the family Theridiidae, also lay eggs early in the summer.)

Diversity (Species Richness/Range
There are around 100 species of running crab spiders in North America. Crab and running crab spiders are among the few families of spiders that are more common in northern climes than in southern areas. In the Carolinas, there are 10 species known to occur (Gaddy and Morse, 1985); (Coyle, 2008).

Running Crab Spiders (Family Philodromidae)

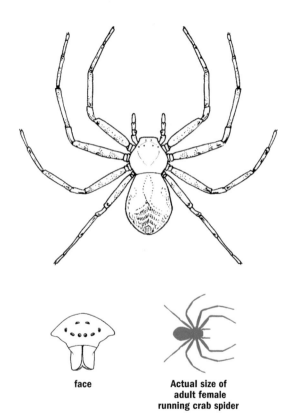

face

Actual size of
adult female
running crab spider

Diamond Spider *Thanatus formicinus*

Found in both grassy areas and in woodlands.

Nature Notes:

Gaddy and Morse (1985) list two species—
T. formicinus and *T. ribicellus* from South Carolina.

Thanatus vulgaris is known from North Carolina and Georgia and is probably overlooked in South Carolina.

Description: The running crab spiders have legs nearly the same length. Legs II and IV are only slightly longer than the other legs. They are brown to gray, relatively drab-colored spiders, with black markings. *Thanatus formicinus* has a distinctive dark diamond on the abdomen ↑. North American *Thanatus* spp. females may be as long as 10 mm while the males are up to 6 mm.

Web & Hunting Technique: These spiders generally camouflage themselves on gravel, brown grasses, tree bark or Spanish moss (see Howell and Jenkins, 2004) and are rarely seen on flowers.

Life Cycle: : Overwinters as subadult; mating occurs in late spring.

Range: *Thanatus formicinus* is found throughout the United States, according to Kaston (1978).

Dutton Slender Crab Spider *Tibellus duttoni*

Broomsedge fields (Barnes and Barnes, 1955), pastures, woods edges and savannahs.

Description: This spider doesn't really look much like a crab spider, except for the fact that Leg II is longer than Leg I in this species. The general color is gray to brown with a thin, brown band down the middle of the spider's body ↑ and a pair of spots ↑. The distinctive feature of this spider is its thin abdomen, which is thinner that its cephalothorax. Females 6 to 10 mm; males 5 to 7 mm.

Web & Hunting Technique: Camouflages itself by extending legs in line with its body (as in longjawed orbweavers). It looks like part of the twig upon which it is sitting and can quickly pounce on insects from this position.

Life Cycle: Matures in summer to late summer, hatches from egg sac in spring.

Range: Sporadic throughout the Carolinas; probably overlooked. Eastern United States west to Texas and Minnesota.

Nature Notes:

Rymal and Folkerts (1982) found this spider in the pitchers of pitcher-plants (*Sarracenia* spp.), possibly using the plants for prey capture and nesting.

Coyle (2008) lists eight species of *Philodromus*, a more northern genus of this family, from the Smokies.

Crab Spiders
Family Thomisidae

Description
The crab spiders are small to medium-sized spiders generally ranged from 5 to 10 mm in body length. Legs I-III are curved and shaped like those of crabs. The abdomen is triangular-shaped with a rounded base or posterior end.

Similar Spiders
The closely-related philodromids are the only spiders that resemble the crab spiders. They are, however, climbers and move faster than the thomisids. The Spinybacked Orbweaver, *Gasteracantha cancriformis*, is sometimes called "Crab Spinyback" or simply "Crab Spider," but it is a true orbweaver that has an abdomen that is spiny and crab-shaped. An examination of its legs, however, reveals that it is not a true crab spider.

Habitat
In fields, savannahs, and meadows primarily. These spiders are closely associated with flowers that are found in open areas.

Hunting Techniques/Web
Crab spiders are sit-and-wait hunters. They camouflage themselves on a flower and wait until the predator—usually a flying pollinator—comes along. Their prey is mostly small bees and other insects, but they have been known to kill large butterflies.

Eggs and Egg Sac
Egg sacs are flat and attached to nearby stems or twigs. The female guards the eggs until she dies.

Observations
These colorful spiders are famous for their ability to camouflage themselves on brightly-colored (usually yellowish to white) flowers and have the ability to change colors when necessary.

Diversity (Species Richness/Range)
There are around 120 species of crab spiders in North America. There are over 20 species of crab spiders known to occur in the Carolinas (Gaddy and Morse, 1985); (Coyle, 2008).

Crab Spiders (Family Thomisidae)

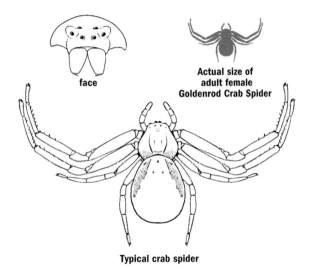

face

**Actual size of
adult female
Goldenrod Crab Spider**

Typical crab spider

Goldenrod Crab Spider *Misumena vatia*

Found on flowers, usually in meadows, fields, savannahs and other non-forested areas.

Nature Notes:

This spider and the Whitebanded Crab Spider have the ability to change body color to match the flower upon which they are sitting in wait.

Description: This bright crab spider is one of the most well-known and distinctive of all spiders. Females are chalk-white to yellow to yellowish brown—the eye region of the carapace of the cephalothorax is always whitish. The abdomen is often unmarked but occasionally shows two pinkish stripes ↑ down the sides. Males are usually light to dark brown with Legs I and II very dark brown (Legs III and IV are often clear). Females are 6 to 9 mm in length; males are 3 to 4 mm.

Web & Hunting Technique: The Goldenrod Crab Spider is a sit-and-wait hunter. It camouflages itself on a white to yellow flower and waits for a pollinator or nectar thief to land on the flower. When an insect lands, the spider pounces on it quickly. While holding the prey, the spider bites the back of its neck piercing the nerve ganglia and paralyzing the insect.

Males don't look anything like the females—and they are much smaller (See size bars on opposite page).

Life Cycle: Matures in summer to late summer, hatches from egg sac in spring.

Range: Common throughout the Carolinas. Found throughout the United States and Canada.

Goldenrod Crab Spiders are patient hunters. This one has captured a crescent butterfly.

Whitebanded Crab Spider *Misumenoides formosipes*

F

M

♀

Found on bright yellow and white flowers in non-forested areas.

Nature Notes:

The incurved shape of Legs I and II gives these spiders the appearance of crabs.

They are not to be confused with the Spinybacked Orbweaver (*Gasteracantha cancriformis*).

Description: The Whitebanded Crab Spider is also called the Flower Spider. Like the Goldenrod Crab Spider, it is generally yellow, white or brownish in color. Unlike the Goldenrod Crab Spider, it usually has red or brown markings on the sides and top of the abdomen ↑. The abdomen often tapers to a point. There is a row of white bands or ridges around the eye region ↑. Females are 5 to 11 mm in length; males are 2.5 to 3.5 mm.

Web & Hunting Technique: The Whitebanded Crab Spider can convincingly camouflage itself on white and yellow flowers. There it waits for an insect to land on the flower. When the insect lands, the spider pounces on it quickly. While holding the prey, the spider bites the back of its neck piercing the nerve ganglia and paralyzing the insect.

Though Whitebanded Crab Spiders are occasionally found on pink and purple flowers, their camouflage is most effective on white or yellow flowers.

Egg Sac & Eggs: Egg sac is silken white and holds up to 100 eggs (Howell and Jenkins, 2004).

Life Cycle: Matures in late summer and fall; emerges from egg sac in spring.

Range: This is the most common crab spider in the Carolinas, where it is abundant. Found throughout the United States and Canada.

Tan Crab Spider *Xysticus transversatus*

Woods, fields, shrubby areas and around houses.

Nature Notes:

There are 11 species of *Xysticus* reported from South Carolina; the Tan Crab Spider is the most common of these.

Coyle (2008) lists eight *Xysticus* species from the Smokies.

Description: The crab spiders of the genus *Xysticus* are generally duller in color than other thomisids. The Tan Crab Spider is tan to reddish-brown and has a flattened abdomen with three to four pairs of light and dark bands ↑. The abdomen also has parallel grooves or dimples often between the color bands. Males have banded rear legs. Cephalothorax has a wide light band down the middle ↑ bordered by a pair of very dark bands. Females are 6 to 7 mm in length; males are 5 to 6 mm long.

Web & Hunting Technique: A well-camouflaged sit-and-wait hunter.

Egg Sac & Eggs: Eggs are laid in silken retreats, often in folded leaves.

Life Cycle: Overwinters as subadult; mating occurs in late spring.

Range: New England south to Georgia and west to the Rockies. Common throughout the Carolinas.

Xysticus species can come in several shades of drab. This yellowish specimen is as bright as they get.

A close up look at the face and eye pattern of a *Xysticus* crab spider.

Jumping Spiders
Family Salticidae

Description
The jumping spiders are short, stout, hairy spiders with two extremely large eyes and six smaller ones. They are relatively small to medium sized spiders and hunt primarily in the daytime. And, as their name indicates, they jump about from place to place and are very active spiders.

Similar Spiders
No other spiders look like jumping spiders. Jumping spiders, however, often mimic ants (remember, spiders have eight legs; ants have only six).

This jumping spider has better vision than most spiders. Note the prominent anterior median eyes.

Habitat
In fields, savannahs, meadows, woods edges, woodlands, around buildings, in cities and in houses. Jumping spiders, however, are somewhat rarer than some other spider families in forests.

Hunting Techniques/Web
Jumping spiders have excellent eyesight. They hunt by day. They can stalk prey, estimate distances and pounce on the prey when ready to attack. They do not build snares, but do make silken retreats.

Eggs Sacs and Eggs
Egg sac is usually produced inside a retreat where female guards the eggs until they hatch.

Observations
Jumping spiders are fun to watch. They actually seem to look directly at you from time to time. They will jump onto an outstretched hand (without biting it). They perform interesting courtship rituals that involve the waving of their first legs. And, with their iridescence, they are among the most colorful and photogenic of all spiders.

Diversity (Species Richness/Range)
There are around 300 species of jumping spiders in North America. Steve Roach, an arachnologist/entomologist from Florence, South Carolina, has reported over 60 species of jumping spiders from the state (Roach and Edwards, 1984). The Smokies have 55 species (Coyle, 2008).

Jumping Spiders (Family Salticidae)

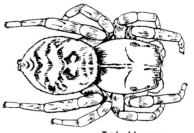

Typical jumper

face

Actual size range of adult female jumpers

Bronze Jumper *Eris militaris (= E. marginata)*

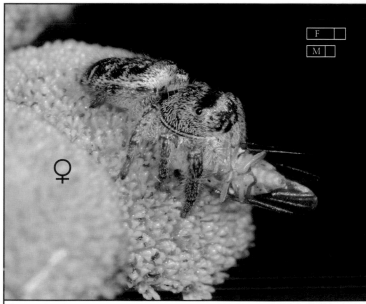

F

M

♀

Low shrubs, cypress swamps, rock outcrops and woodland edges.

Nature Notes:

This jumping spider has been known by both *Eris militaris* and *Eris marginata*. Platnick (2008) gives *militaris* as the preferred specific name.

Males of this species closely resemble those of *Marpissa lineata*. *Marpissa lineata*, however-er, is a darker species with more prominent white lines on the abdomen. Furthermore, in *M. lineata*, Leg II is shorter than in *Eris militaris* and Leg I is longer.

Description: Female is a hairy gray spider with a salt and pepper look; male is a bronze-brown with few hairs and lighter bands bordering each side of the abdomen and cephalothorax ↑. Females are from 6 to 8 mm long; males are 4 to 7 mm in length.

Web & Hunting Technique: No web is built. Pursue and pounce on prey.

Life Cycle: No data available.

Range: Reported from the Piedmont and Coastal Plain of South Carolina (Gaddy and Morse, 1984), and from the Great Smoky Mountains of North Carolina (Coyle, 2008). Ranges throughout the United States (Kaston, 1978).

Males are more boldly marked than females—and with fewer hairs.

Note the large chelicerae on this male.

No need for a straw; jumpers suck the liqui-fied insides of prey out with their mouth and the aid of their sucking stomach.

Hentz Longjawed Jumper *Hentzia palmarum*

♀

Many habitats: soybean fields, grassy areas, palmetto trees, shrubs, deciduous forest and rock outcrops.

Nature Notes:

Also known as *Hentzia ambigua.*

Howell and Jenkins (2004) give trees, shrubs, and low grasses as habitats; Roach and Edwards (1984) say the species is found in "low shrubs" and "soybeans." Collection sites of specimens include apple trees, rock outcrops, soybean fields, deciduous forest, palmetto trees, grassy fields, etc.

Description: The males of Hentz Longjawed Jumper have extremely long chelicerae ("jaws") ↑, often over half the length of the cephalothorax. Leg I is unusually long and dark brown in color. In the female, lacks the long jaws and often has clear or light-colored legs. Nondescript chevron patterns on the abdomen. Females are 4.7 to 6 mm in length; males are 3.7 to 5.5 mm.

Web & Hunting Technique: A sit-and-wait or pursue-and-pounce hunter like most jumpers.

Life Cycle: Active year round on warm days.

Range: Listed as "common" in South Carolina in Gaddy and Morse (1985). Frequently collected in the Carolinas based on the number of extant specimens. Found from Canada south to Florida and west to Oklahoma and Nebraska.

Like all Jumpers, this Hentz Longjawed Jumper has captured prey without the aid of a web. They watch and pounce. Also note his extremely long chelicerae or jaws.

Magnolia Green Jumper *Lyssomanes viridis*

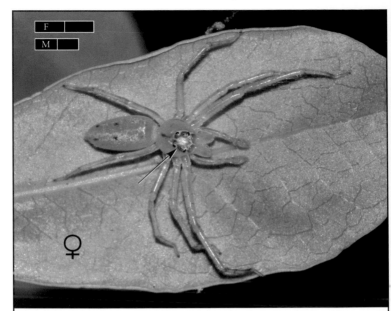

F

M

♀

Found primarily in shrubby and forested areas where it camouflages itself on leaves.

Nature Notes:

The Magnolia Green Jumper is a member of a tropical genus known throughout the New World Tropics.

The Magnolia Green Jumper is abundant in dense wetlands and on barrier islands.

It is a spectacular spider to watch. Due to its light weight, jumping ability and the complex silk lines it uses, the Magnolia Green Jumper seems to bounce from leaf to leaf, the leaves unmoved.

Description: The Magnolia Green Jumper (or simply "Magnolia Jumper") is one of the easiest North American jumping spiders to identify. Females are bright green with several pairs of black spots on the abdomen's dorsum. Males are brownish to greenish with dorsal spots and/or stripes. Both sexes have a distinctive raised "eye mound" ringed with orange ↑ (with black tubercles) on the cephalothorax. [Some taxonomists put this genus in a separate family of jumping spiders—the Lyssomanidae —because of the arrangement of its eyes.] Males have strikingly large chelicerae. Females are 7 to 8 mm in length; males are 5 to 6 mm.

Web & Hunting Technique: No web is built. Pursue and pounce on prey.

Life Cycle: Immatures of this species are unusually abundant in early spring in South Carolina, probably indicating that it overwin-

If it weren't for the backlighting, this Magnolia Green Jumper would be nearly invisible.

ters as a subadult. Berry (1971) found immatures abundant in October and November in the Piedmont of North Carolina.

Range: North to North Carolina, west to Texas, common in the New World tropics. In South Carolina, it is found statewide, but is much more common in the Coastal Plain.

Eyes are able to move independently as can be seen in this image. Also note the orange "eye mound."

Pike Slender Jumper *Marpissa pikei (=Hyctia p.)*

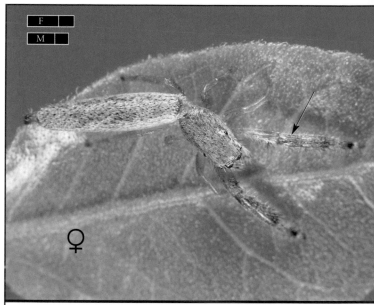

F

M

♀

Fields, grasslands and woodlands.

Nature Notes:

The Pike Slender Jumper is extremely quick for its size and jumps unbelievable distances.

Howell and Jenkins (2004) found it to be a voracious eater in captivity.

Description: The Pike Slender Jumper does not really look like a jumping spider upon first observation. Unlike most jumping spiders, it has a narrow, elongate body, more than three times as long as wide. This jumper's coloration is highly variable and ranges from powdery grey to brown. The male's abdomen has a dark band bordered in white down its middle ↑. Legs I ↑ are often held straight up or out in front of the spider and are used less for walking than for prey gathering and eating. Females are 6 to 9 mm in length; males are 6 to 8 mm.

Marpissa lineata, its congener, is also common in South Carolina, according to Roach & Edwards (1984). It has a broader cephalothorax than *M. pikei*, and has a pair of parallel white lines on both the ventral and dorsal surfaces of its abdomen. Females of *M. lineata* are only 4 to 5.3 mm long, while males are 3 to 4 mm.

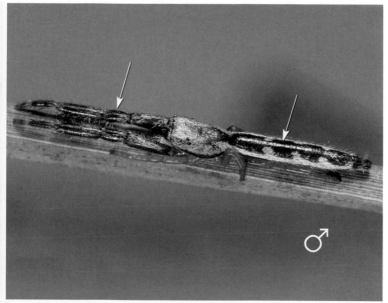

This male is camouflaging himself by stretching out along a piece of stem. An unwary insect may not notice this dangerous predator before it is too late.

Web & Hunting Technique: Hunts by eyesight and speed. No web is built.

Life Cycle: No data available.

Range: It is common on the barrier islands of South Carolina (Gaddy and Morse, 1985), and Barnes and Barnes (1955) found abundant in Piedmont broomsedge (*Andropogon virginicus*) fields in North Carolina. Eastern North America west to Nebraska and Arizona. Common throughout the Carolinas.

Dimorphic Jumper *Maevia inclemens (=M. vittata)*

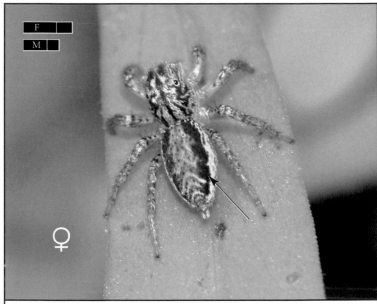

F

M

♀

Buildings, woodlands, shrubby areas, residential areas and grassy fields.

Nature Notes:

The Dimorphic Jumper is one of those extraordinarily alert species of jumpers. Howell and Jenkins (2004) noted that "it is a curious spider and shows great deal of interest in its collector."

♂

"Dimorphic" means that males and females have different shapes or colors. This is a black form male.

Description: This spider gets its name from the dimorphic males, which vary in coloration from gray with reddish lateral bands on the abdomen to completely black with white legs. The abdomen in females is grey to brown with iridescent reddish lateral bands ↑. Females are 6.5 to 10 mm in length; males are 5 to 7 mm.

Web & Hunting Technique: Hunts by eyesight and speed. No web is built.

Life Cycle: Probably overwinters as adult—Adults have been collected in South Carolina in March (Gaddy and Morse, 1985).

Range: Eastern North America west to Texas and Wisconsin. Common throughout the Carolinas.

Orange Jumper *Paraphidippus aurantia*

♂

| F | |
| M | |

Low shrubs, grasses.

Description: The female of this species has an greenish-bronze abdomen with an orange marginal line. The males are black with a white marginal line around the abdomen and have large chelicerae and abundant hair on Leg I. Females are from 8 to 12 mm long; males are 7 to 10 mm.

Web & Hunting Technique: Hunts by eyesight and speed. No web is built.

Egg Sac & Eggs: Often found in silken tube in folded leaves.

Life Cycle: No data available.

Range: North Carolina south to Florida and across the Gulf States to Texas (Kaston, 1978). Roach and Edwards (1984) indicate that this species occurs north to Virginia but only along the immediate coast.

Nature Notes:

This jumping spider was previously known as *Eris aurantia*, but has been assigned to the genus *Paraphidippus* in Platnick (2008).

Apache Jumper *Phidippus apacheanus*

F

M

Forested and non-forested habitats.

Nature Notes:

The Apache Jumper appears to be a more southern species of *Phidippus*, not having been collected north of Maryland.

A striking spider, *Phidippus apacheanus* sports red above and contrasting green chelicerae.

Description: The Apache Jumper is yellow to reddish-orange with few markings on its abdomen or cephalothorax. It can be confused with the more red *Phidippus cardinalis*, and it is often mistaken for *Phidippus whitmanii* (Whitman Jumper), which has white markings on its abdomen. Females are from 11 to 12 mm long; males are 9 to 11 mm.

Web & Hunting Technique: Hunts by eyesight and speed. No web is built.

Egg Sac & Eggs: In most *Phidippus* species, the male guards the egg sac, which is laid in late summer and fall.

Life Cycle: Little is known of the life cycle of this species.

Range: Maryland and Pennsylvania south to Florida and west to California (Kaston, 1978).

Bold Jumper *Phidippus audax*

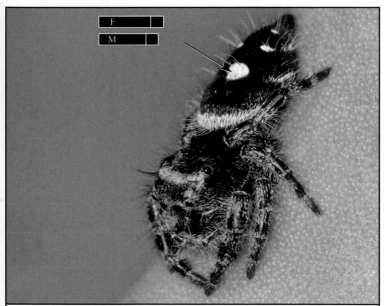

Forests, agricultural fields, grassy areas and in and around buildings.

Description: The Bold Jumper is probably the largest jumping spider in the Carolinas. It is a large, predominantly black, hairy spider. The abdomen has one large, triangular white spot ↑, with two smaller white spots just below (these spots are sometimes reddish to orange in immature individuals). The primary eyes are extremely large, and the chelicerae are iridescent green ↑. Females are from 8 to 15 mm long; males are 12 to 13 mm.

Web & Hunting Technique: Hunts by eyesight and speed. No web is built.

Life Cycle: Known to overwinter in retreat made from leaves and silk or under stones (Comstock, 1965).

Range: Eastern North America to Canada and west to California. Common throughout the Carolinas, but more abundant in the Coastal Plain.

Nature Notes:

As its name indicates, this is an aggressive spider, often waving its front legs into the air in territorial (and sexual) displays.

A friend once called to say she had a "bug" of some sort attacking her. I arrived to find a large male *Phidippus audax* defending his territory, which he surmised to be her entire porch.

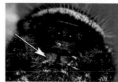

The iridescent green chelicerae shine when the light hits them.

Brilliant Jumper *Phidippus clarus (=P. rimator)*

F
M
♂

A variety of non-forested habitats: tall grasses, bushes, broomsedge fields.

Nature Notes:

Generally found in a variety of non-forested habitats. Roach and Edwards (1984) note that this spider is most common in the "herb-shrub" zone in eastern [Coastal Plain] South Carolina. Kaston (1978) gives the habitat as "tall grasses and bushes." Barnes and Barnes (1955) found it to be the most common jumping spider of broomsedge (*Andropogon virginicus*)-dominated fields in North Carolina.

Description: The male Brilliant Jumper has a black or brownish cephalothorax and a reddish-orange abdomen. It can be distinguished from most other red or orange *Phidippus* species by the presence of a wide black band ↑ down the abdomen and the all black cephalothorax. Females are more drab with an orangeish abdomen marked with two longitudinal black stripes and three pairs of white spots ↑. Females are from 8 to 10 mm long; males are 5 to 7 mm in length.

Web & Hunting Technique: Hunts by eyesight and speed. No web is built.

Egg Sac & Eggs: In most *Phidippus* species, the male guards the egg sac, which is laid in late summer and fall. In *P. clarus*, according to Howell and Jenkins (2004), the egg sac is laid in silken cocoon placed in a folded leaf.

Females are much more drab than the gaudily adorned males.

Life Cycle: Known to overwinter in retreat made from leaves and silk or under stones (Comstock, 1965).

Range: One of the most widely distributed species of the genus *Phidippus*, the Brilliant Jumper is found throughout most of the continental United States and in southern Canada (Kaston, 1978).

This female has retreated into her silken retreat on a milkweed leaf.

Canopy Jumper *Phidippus otiosus*

F

M

♀

Often in trees. Also small shrubs, grasses, bushes, woodlands.

Nature Notes:

Could also be known as the "Lazy" Jumper (from the Latin, *otiosus*=idle)

Howell and Jenkins (2004) list it from a variety of habitats ("small shrubs, bushes, and grasses"), while Roach and Edwards (1984) consider it "the most common woodland species in central and coastal South Carolina, often seen foraging in tree canopies."

Description: The Canopy Jumper is distinctly patterned large jumper and is usually not confused with other species. Its cephalothorax is generally black, but its abdomen is multicolored with a V-shaped orange pattern ↑ pointing toward the cephalothorax. It often has long, white hairs on its legs and body. It often has iridescent chelicerae ↑. Females are from 10 to 15 mm long; males are 9 to 11 mm.

Web & Hunting Technique: Hunts by eyesight and speed. No web is built.

Egg Sac & Eggs: In most *Phidippus* species, the male guards the egg sac, which is laid in late summer and fall.

Life Cycle: No data available.

Range: Maryland south to Florida and west to Texas (Kaston, 1978). Roach and Edwards (1984) note that is more common in central and coastal South Carolina than the rest of the state. Reported from the Smokies by Coyle (2008).

A pair of *Phidippus otiosus* are in the midst of a courtship display (male on right).

Note the beautiful iridescent chelicerae (jaws).

Grayish Jumper *Phidippus princeps*

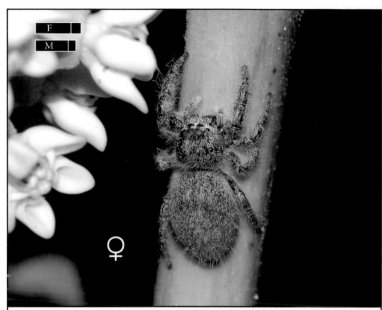

Second growth forests, shrubby areas, disturbed sites.

Nature Notes:

Found in second growth forests and shrubby areas, according to Roach and Edwards (1984), inhabiting areas similar to those preferred by *Phidippus clarus*.

Males are more colorful and with narrower abdomens.

Description: The Grayish Jumper is named for the females; a hairy, often grayish-colored spider with long hairs on its cephalothorax and abdomen. Although it may have patches of orange and brown, the female is usually peppered gray and brown with long hairs. The eyes are nearly black and stand out against the light colored front of the cephalothorax. Males have a black cephalothorax and orange markings on the abdomen. Females are around 10 mm long; males are about 8 mm in length.

Web & Hunting Technique: Hunts by eyesight and speed. No web is built.

Egg Sac & Eggs: In most *Phidippus* species, the male guards the egg sac, which is laid in late summer and fall.

Life Cycle: No data available.

Range: Reported from the Smokies by Coyle (2008). Northeastern states southward to Texas.

Whitman Jumper *Phidippus whitmanii*

Forests, grassy areas, shrubs. Leaf litter in deciduous woods.

Description: Whitman Jumper is reddish-orange with a distinct white band ↑ around the anterior margins of its abdomen and a pair or two of white dashes on the abdomen ↑. It may be confused with *Phidippus apacheanus*, which is entirely unmarked orange on its abdomen and cephalothorax. Females are around 9 mm long, males about 8 mm.

Web & Hunting Technique: Hunts by eyesight and speed. No web is built.

Egg Sac & Eggs: In most *Phidippus* species, the male guards the egg sac, which is laid in late summer and fall.

Life Cycle: May overwinter in retreats made from leaves and silk or under stones.

Range: Found on forest floors throughout most of South Carolina (Roach and Edwards, 1984). New England west to South Dakota and south to Florida. Reported from the Smokies by Coyle (2008).

Nature Notes:

I have seen this spider most commonly in leaf litter in deciduous woods in the Piedmont and the Mountains of the Carolinas.

Howell and Jenkins (2004) found it in "grassy and low herbaceous habitats."

Where's the red? Females have the same pattern as males but are more drab.

Regal Jumper *Phidippus regius*

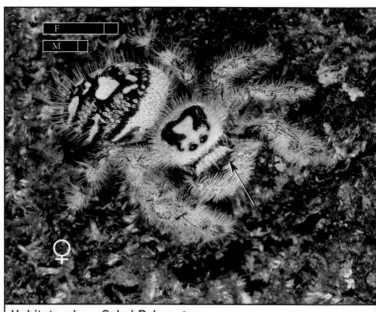

Habitats where Sabal Palms grow.

Nature Notes:

Roach and Edwards (1984) have found this species only where "palmettos [*Sabal palmetto*] occur."

The *Phidippus* jumping spiders, with more than 50 species known, are the most numerous and most conspicuous of the jumping spiders.

Description: The Regal Jumper is a very large and hairy species that has several color varieties; some females are orange (top and middle photos next page) and some are gray-white (top photo this page). Males are mostly black with white markings. The females can be similar in appearance to *Phidippus otiosus*; however, the cephalothorax of *P. regius* has more hairs than that of *P. otiosus* and the abdomen of *P. regius* has fewer and smaller light spots. Chelicerae in females are iridescent pink-violet ↑ and green in males. Females are from 13 to 19 mm long; males are 9 mm.

Web & Hunting Technique: Hunts by eyesight and speed; pouncing on prey. No web is constructed.

Egg Sac & Eggs: In most *Phidippus* species, the male guards the egg sac, which is laid in late summer and fall.

This orange-variety female has captured a fly. It is a testament to jumping spiders stealth and hunting ability that they can capture flies.

Life Cycle: No data available.

Range: North Carolina south to Florida and across the Gulf States to Texas (Kaston, 1978). Roach and Edwards (1984) indicate that this species occurs north to Virginia but only along the immediate coast.

Another orange-variety female showing typical head and abdomen patterns.

A male Regal Jumper makes a tethered leap onto large prey—an unsuspecting grasshopper.

Flat Jumper *Platycryptus undatus (=Metacyrba undata)*

F
M

♀

Wide variety of habitats. Found under bark, on tree trunks [palmettos], in mountain forests and in houses.

Nature Notes:

The Flat Jumper is one of the most common jumping spiders in the Carolinas. It is especially common in and around houses.

Description: The Flat or Familiar Jumper is a somewhat drably-colored, gray to brown, white and black jumper. It has an elongated, flatted body, with a zig-zagged gray band ↑ on a black abdomen. The chelicerae are prominent with long, gray hairs. Also look for the red clypeus ↑ on the females. Females are from 10 to 13 mm long; males are 8 to 10 mm.

Web & Hunting Technique: Hunts by eyesight and speed. No web is built.

Life Cycle: It apparently overwinters as an adult and is frequently seen in houses, especially sunning on windows, in winter.

Range: Found in eastern North America west to Texas and Wisconsin. Abundant throughout the state.

A zig-zagged median band on the abdomen of the Flat Jumper is a useful mark to look for.

♀

Note the red clypeus on this Flat Jumper. The clypeus is defined as the area between the anterior median eyes and the chelicerae.

Pantropic Jumper *Plexippus paykulli*

Most commonly found in port cities on automobiles and in houses and other buildings.

Nature Notes:

As its name indicates, the Pantropic Jumper is what biogeographers call a "cosmotropical" species and is found throughout the warm regions of the world. In Tanzania, it has been called the "Cosmo-tropical Building Spider" due to its habitat of dwelling in man-made structures. It has been collected in Africa, Japan, Hong Kong, Hawaii and New Mexico, and is common in most tropical ports.

It is frequently found on cars and buildings in Savannah and Charleston. It is also common on inhabited barrier islands.

Description: The Pantropic (or Cosmotropical) Jumper is a predominantly gray spider marked more like a wolf spider than a jumper. The male has a parallel pair of broad black bands running the length of its abdomen and cephalothorax. Two white dots ↑ punctuate the dark stripes on the abdomen. Females are much more muted but with the same general coloration. Note that she has a short dark stripe in the middle of the abdomen's light median stripe ↑. Females are from 10 to 12 mm long; males are 10 mm.

Web & Hunting Technique: Hunts by eyesight and speed. No web is built.

Life Cycle: Overwinters as an adult.

Range: Cosmotropical. Common in Charleston and other coastal cities in the Carolinas. Roach and Edwards (1984), however, found it in Clemson, in the northwestern corner of South Carolina.

A hunting female uses her large AMEs (anterior median eyes) to search for prey.

Take the time to study the faces of jumping spiders. Many have spectacular coloration such as this Pantropic Jumper.

Orange Antmimic Jumper *Sarinda hentzii*

Grasses, weeds, hardwood forests, peach orchards—near ants.

Nature Notes:

Sarinda spiders are reddish to black and some species look like carpenter ants (*Camponotus* spp.)

Found in grasses and weeds "in close proximity to streams and ponds" (Howell and Jenkins, 2004), peach orchards (Lee, 1981 in Gaddy and Morse, 1985), and leaf litter in mixed hardwood forests (Roach and Edwards, 1984).

Note that most antmimics are in the Corrinidae family (see page 146).

Description: At first glance, this spider does not appear to be a jumping spider at all. *Sarinda hentzii* is a thin, smooth-bodied jumping spider that mimics ants. A groove/ depression in the cephalothorax ↑ gives it the impression that it has a separate head and thorax like an ant. There is also a depressed groove midway down the abdomen that is usually marked with a white stripe ↑. Adults of both sexes are from 5 to 7 mm in length.

Web & Hunting Technique: These are among the only jumping spiders that don't jump. They are faster than ants, but not as quick as most Salticid spiders. Silk is used to make an overwintering or "hibernation" sac; no web is built to capture prey.

Life Cycle: No data available.

Range: Roach & Edwards (1984) thought this species "rare" or undercollected in the Coastal Plain of South Carolina. Present in the Smokies (Coyle, 2008). North to Maine.

Formica Antmimic Jumper *Synemosyna formica*

Peach orchards, dry leaf litter, houses, swamps—near ants.

Description: *Synemosyna formica* is a thin, smooth-bodied jumping spider that mimics ants. *Synemosyna* individuals are usually reddish (though rarely black females are seen) and resemble *Formica* ants. Adults are 5 to 7 mm in length.

Web & Hunting Technique: These are probably among the only jumping spiders that don't "jump." They are faster than ants, but not as quick as most Salticid spiders.

Silk is used in the construction of an overwintering or "hibernation" sac; no web is built to capture prey.

Life Cycle: Along the coast, these spiders probably overwinter in leaf litter or in grassy areas. In the Piedmont and Mountains, they probably hibernate in sacs.

Range: Sporadic or overlooked in the Carolinas. Known from New England south to Florida and west to Texas and Kansas.

Nature Notes:

Spiders of a closely related genus, *Peckhamia,* are smaller and more wide-bodied and mimic several species of ants, notably *Crematogaster* or acrobat ants.

The resemblance to a *Formica* ant is uncanny. This trait helps the spider hunt unnoticed among ants.

Glossary

Abdomen: The posterior portion of a spider body.

ALE: Anterior lateral eyes.

AME: Anterior median eyes.

Anal Tubercle: Small projection at the posterior end of the abdomen on which the anus opens.

Annulated: Showing rings of pigmentation, as on a leg. Ringed or banded.

Anterior: Toward the front.

Appendages: Structures extending away from the body proper; for example, legs, palps, etc.

Arachnida: Class in the phylum Arthropoda that includes spiders, harvestmen, ticks, mites, scorpions, whipscorpions, windscorpions and pseudoscorpions.

Arachnology: The scientific study of arachnids (including spiders).

Araneae: The arachnid order of spiders.

Araneologist: A biologist who specializes in the study of spiders.

Araneomorphae: One of the two infraorders of spiders (the other is Mygalomorphae). Most true spiders are in this group

Book lung: A respiratory organ with page-like folds that is found in most spiders.

Calamistrum: A series of curved bristles on the fourth leg of some spiders (cribellate spiders). Used to comb out silk threads for prey capture.

Carapace: Top of the cephalothorax. The fused series of sclerites making up the dorsal part of the cephalothorax.

Caudal: The posterior end.

Cephalothorax: The anterior of the two major divisions into which the body of a spider is divided. It is the head and thorax combined.

Cervical groove: The furrow which extends forward and toward the sides from the center of the carapace and marks the boundary between the head and the thorax. It is sometimes indistinct or completely lacking.

Chelicerae: The jaws; consisting of a pair of stout basal segments each with a terminal fang.

Claw: A strong curved process at the distal end of the leg.

Claw tufts: The bunch of hairs at the tip of the tarsus in those spiders with only two claws.

Clypeus: The region or the cephalothorax between the anterior eyes and the chelicerae.

Comb: Bristles with barbs on tarsus 4 in members of the family Theridiidae. Used to "comb out" silk onto prey.

Coxa: The segment of the leg (or pedipalp) nearest the body.

Cribellate: Adjective referring to a spider that possesses a cribellum.

Cribellum: A silk-spinning, transverse, plate-like organ in front of the spinnerets in cribellate spiders. It produces the hackled band silk threads.

Denticle: A small, smooth tooth, usually on chelicerae, legs or palps.

Distal: At the opposite end of the point of attachment.

Dorsal: Situated near the top or above other sections.

Dorsal Furrow: A median groove, depression or pigmented line behind the cervical groove on the carapace.

Dorsum: The back, or upper surface, of the spider.

Ecribellate: Adjective referring to a spider that does not possess a cribellum.

Egg Sac: Spider eggs enclosed in a silk casing.

Endite: One of the mouth parts; ventral to the mouth opening and lateral to the lip, so that in chewing it opposes the chelicerae.

Entomophagous: Feeding on insects. Spiders are entomophagous.

Exuviae: The cast off "skin" of a molting spider. The old exoskeleton of an arthropod.

Fangs: Claw-like segments on the spider's chelicerae. Used to inject poison.

Femur: The third segment of the pedipalp or leg, counting from nearest the body.

Folium: Pigmented pattern on the abdomen, often shaped like an oak leaf. Common in the Araneidae orbweavers.

Hub: Central area of a web; as in an orb web where the radial threads converge.

Immature: A non-adult spider.

Instar: The stage of the immature spider between successive molts.

Kleptoparasite: A spider that steals prey caught by another spider.

Labium: The lower lip between the two endites of spiders.

Laterigrade: A sideways type of locomotion; as in the crab spiders and their allies. Also, the way the legs are turned in on these spiders so that the dorsal surface is posterior.

Lung Slits: External openings to the book lungs; located along the epigastric furrow.

Metatarsus: The sixth segment of the leg or pedipalp, counting from nearest the body.

Mygalimorphae: One of the two infraorders of spiders (the other is Mygalomorphae). Members include the tarantulas and trapdoor spiders.

Ocular Quadrangle: The area on the carapace enclosed by the two rows of eyes.

Opisthosoma: The posterior body region of a spider. Another name for the abdomen.

Orb: A web consisting of radial strands on which spiral or circular threads are arranged in a single plane. The stereotypical spider web.

Palp: The segments of the pedipalp distal to the endite or coxa. In females it resembles a leg; in males it is modified for sperm transfer.

Patella: The fourth segment of the leg or pedipalp, counting from nearest the body.

Pedicel: The small stalk connecting the abdomen to the cephalothorax.

Pedipalp: The second appendage of the cephalothorax, behind the chelicerae but in front of the legs. They are tipped with the palp bulb.

PLE: Posterior lateral eyes.

PME: Posterior median eyes.

Posterior: Rear end; or toward the rear.

Prosoma: The anterior body region of a spider. Another name for the cephalothorax.

Proximal: The point of attachment of an appendage; or toward it.

Recurved: A curved arc such that the ends are nearer to the posterior of the body than its center.

Retromargin: The margin of the cheliceral fang furrow farther from the front of the body, nearer the endite.

Scopula: A brush of hairs on the lower surface of the tarsus and metatarsus in some spiders.

Scutum: A sclerotized plate; as on the abdomen of some spiders.

Spinnerets: The silk-spinning, paired appendages on the end of the abdomen. There are six.

Spinose: Provided with spines.

Spiracle: The opening of the tubular tracheae on the ventral side of the abdomen.

Spur: A cuticular process; heavier than a spine.

Spurious Claws: The serrated bristles at the end of the tarsus.

Stabilimentum: The bands of silk spun by certain orb-weavers in webs; often zigzag.

Sternum: The central plate on the underside of the cephalothorax of a spider.

Tarsus: The last segment of the leg or pedipalp, counting from nearest the body.

Thorax: That portion of the cephalothorax posterior to the cervical groove.

Tibia: The fifth segment of the leg or pedipalp, counting from nearest the body.

Tracheae: Tubes through which air is carried inside the body of the spider and which open at the spiracle.

Trichobothria: A fine sensory hair protruding at a right angle from the leg.

Trochanter: The second segment of the leg or pedipalp, counting from nearest the body.

Tubercle: A low, usually rounded, process.

Venter: The underside of the spider.

Ventral: Situated underneath or below other sections.

References & Selected Reading

Abbot, John. 1792. *Spiders of Georgia*. Drawings and notes in the form of a manuscript. London.

Barnes, R. D. and B. M. Barnes. 1955. *The Spider Population of the Abstract Broomsedge Community*. Ecology 36:658-656.

Berry, J. W. 1970. *Spiders of the North Carolina Piedmont Old Field Communities*. Journal Elisha Mitchell Scientific Society 41:165-212.

Berry, J. W. 1971. *Seasonal Distribution of Common Spiders in the North Carolina Piedmont*. American Midland Naturalist 85:526-531.

Bishop, S. C. and C. R. Crosby. 1926. *Notes on the Spiders of the Southeastern United States with Descriptions of New Species*. Journal of the Elisha Mitchell Scientific Society 41:165-212.

Breene, R. G. 2003. *Common Names of Arachnids*. The American Arachnological Society Committee on Common Names of Arachnids. http://www.americanarachnology.org/acn5.pdf.

Carico, J. E. 1973. *The Nearctic Species of the Genus Dolomedes (Araneae: Pisauridae)*. Bulletin of the Museum of Comparative Zoology 144:435-488.

Chamberlin, R. V. and W. Ivie. 1944. *Spiders of the Georgia Region of North America*. Bulletin of the University of Utah 35:1-267.

Chamberlin, R. V. and W. Ivie. 1947. *Spiders of Alaska*. Bulletin of the University of Utah 37:1-103.

Comstock, J. H. 1965. *The Spider Book* (revised by W. J. Gertsch). Comstock Press. Ithaca, NY.

Coyle, F. A. 1981. *The Mygalomorph genus Microhexura (Araneae, Dipluridae)*. Bulletin of the American Museum of Natural History 170: 64-75.

Coyle, F. A. 2006. *Spiders of the Great Smoky Mountains National Park*. Unpublished list. Cullowhee, North Carolina.

Coyle, F. A. 2008. *Spiders of the Great Smoky Mountains National Park*. http://www.dlia.org.

Coyle, F. A. and A. C. McGarity. 1991. *Two new species of Nesticus spiders from the southern Appalachians (Araneae, Nesticidae)*. Journal of Arachnology 19:161-168.

Crawford, R. L. 1988. *An Annotated Checklist of the Spiders of Washington*. Burke Museum of Natural History. Seattle.

Dean, D. A. 2007. *Spiders of Texas*. http://www.pecanspiders.tamu.edu/spidersoftexas.htm.

Dorris, P. R. 1967. *Spiders of Mississippi*. Ph. D. Dissertation, University of Mississippi, Oxford.

Dorris, P. R. 2007. *An Updated Checklist of the Spiders of Arkansas*. http://www.ezclick.net/pdorris/.

Draney, M. L. 1987. *Ground-layer Spiders of a Georgia Piedmont Agroecosystem: Species Lists, Phenology, and Habitat Selection*. Journal of Arachnology 25:333-351.

Edwards, G. B. and D. E. Hill. 1978. *Representatives of the North American Salticid (Araneae:Salticidae) Fauna.* Peckhamia 1:110-117.

Emerton, J. H. 1961. *Common Spiders of the United States* (revised edition). Dover Books, New York.

Folkerts, D. R. 2006. *A Preliminary Checklist of the Spiders of Alabama.* http://www.auburn.edu/folkedr/spiders/.

Forster, R. R., N. I. Platnick, and M. R. Gray. 1987. *A Review of the Spider Superfamilies Hypochilodea and Austrohypochiloidea (Aranea: Araneomorphae).* Bulletin of the Am. Museum of Natural History 1:1-116.

Gaddy, L. L. 1981. *Observations on Some Maritime Forest Spiders of Four South Carolina Barrier Islands.* Brimleyana 6:159-162.

Gaddy, L. L. and J. C. Morse. 1985. *Common Spiders of South Carolina with an Annotated Checklist.* Technical Bulletin 1094. South Carolina Agricultural Experiment Station. Clemson, South Carolina.

Gaddy, L. L. 1987. *Orbweavers Abundance in Three Forested Communities in the Southern Appalachian Mountains of South Carolina.* Journal of Arachnology 15:273-275.

Gertsch, W. J. 1979. *American Spiders.* Second Edition. Van Nostrand-Reinhold, New York.

Gertsch, W. J. 1984. *The Spider family Nesticidae (Araneae) in North America, Central America, and the West Indies.* Texas Memorial Museum Bulletin 31:1-91.

Hentz, N. M. 1821. *A Notice Concerning the Spider whose Web is used in Medicine.* Journal of the Philadelphia Academy of Natural Sciences II:53-55.

Hillyard, P. 1994. *The Book of the Spider: From Arachnophobia to Love of Spiders.* Random House, New York.

Howard, L. O. 1883. *A List of the Invertebrate Fauna of South Carolina* (Araneae identifications by G. Marx), IN Chapter 11, pp. 265-311, *South Carolina—Its Resources, and Populations, Institutions and Industries.* South Carolina State Board of Agriculture. Walker, Evans, and Cogswell, Charleston.

Howell, W. M. and R. L. Jenkins. 2004. *Spiders of the Eastern United States: A Photographic Guide.* Pearson Education. Boston. 363 p.

Kaston, B. J. 1981. *Spiders of Connecticut* (a revision of 1970 publication). Bulletin of Connecticut State Geological and Natural History Survey 70:1-1020.

Kaston, B. J. 1978. *How to Know the Spiders.* Third Edition. Wm. Brown. Dubuque, IA.

Jackman, J. A. 1999. *A Field guide to the Spiders and Scorpions of Texas.* Lone Star Books, Houston.

Kelley, R. W. 1979. *Niche Partitioning Among Spiders of a Granitic Outcrop.* M. S. Thesis, Clemson University. Clemson, SC.

Lee, G. T. 1981. *Seasonal Abundance of Arthropods on Peach Trees in South Carolina.* Ph. D. Dissertation. Clemson University, Clemson, SC.

Levi, H. W. 1973. *Small Orbweavers of the Genus Araneus (Araneae: Araneidae) North of Mexico.* Bulletin Museum of Comparative Zoology 145:473-552.

Levi, H. W. 1976. *The Orbweaver genera Verrucosa, Acanthepeira, Wagneriana, Acacesia, Wixia, Scoloderus, and Alpaida North of Mexico (Araneae: Araneidae).* Bulletin of the Museum of Comparative Zoology 147:351-391.

Levi, H. W. and H. M. Field. 1954. *Spiders of Wisconsin*. American Midland Naturalist 51:440-467.

Levi, H. W., L. R. Levi, and H. S. Zim. 1990. *Spiders and their Kin*. Golden Press. New York.

Majeski, J. A. and G. G. Durst. 1975. *Bite by the Spider Herpyllus ecclesiasticus in South Carolina*. Toxicon 13:377.

Moulder, B. 1992. *A Guide to the Common Spiders of Illinois*. Illinois State Museum. Springfield.

Pendleton, W. G. 1974. *A synecological Study of the Spiders of the Santee Swamp*. M. S. Thesis. University of South Carolina. Columbia.

Platnick, N. I. 2007. *The World Spider Catalog*. Version 7.5. American Museum of Natural History. http://research.amnh.org/entomology/spiders/catalog/index.html.

Rea, P. M. and L. M. Bragg. 1909. *Local Fauna, Spiders*. Bulletin Charleston Museum 5:65-66.

Reiskind, J. 1969. *The Spider Subfamily Castianeirinae in North America and Central America*. Bulletin Museum of Comparative Zoology 138:163-325.

Richman, D. B. and B. Cutler. 1978. *List of the Jumping Spiders (Araneae:Salticidae) of the United States and Canada*. Peckhamia 1:82-109.

Roach, S. H. 1988. *Reproductive Periods of Phidippus (Araneae: Salticidae) in South Carolina*. Journal of Arachnology 16:95-101.

Roach, S. H. and G. B. Edwards. 1984. *An Annotated List of South Carolina Salticidae (Araneae)*. Peckhamia 2:49-57.

Roth, V. D. 1985. *Spider Genera of North America*. American Arachnological Society. Gainesville, FL.

Rymal, D. E. and G. W. Folkerts. 1982. *Insects Associated with Pitcher Plants and their Relationship with Pitcher Plant Conservation*. Journal of the Alabama Academy of Science 53:131-151.

Sabath, L. E. 1969. *Color Change and Life History of the Spider* Gea heptagon. Psyche 76:367-374.

Turnbull, A. L. 1973. *The Ecology of True Spiders*. Annual Review of Entomology 18:305-348.

Ubick, D., P. Paquin, P.E. Cushing and V. Roth (eds.) 2005. *Spiders of North American: An Identification Manual*. American Arachnological Soc.

U. S. Fish and Wildlife Service. 2008. *Spruce-fir Moss Spider*. www.fws.gov/nces/spider/sprummoss.html.

Weber, L. 2003. *Spiders of the North Woods*. Kollath-Stensaas Publishing. Duluth, MN.

Wharton, C. H., V. W. Lambour, J. Newson, P. V. Winger, L. L. Gaddy, and R. Mancke. 1981. *The Fauna of Bottomland Hardwoods in the Southeastern United States*, pp. 87-160, IN J. R. Clark and J. Benforado, editors, *Proceedings of a workshop on southeastern United States forested wetlands*. Developments in Agriculture and Managed Forest Ecology, vol. II. Elsevier, New York.

Wolff, Robert J. 2008. *Coyle's Purseweb Spider*. South Carolina Department of Natural Resources, Columbia, SC. 3 p. www.dnr.sc.gov/cwcs/pdf/Pursewebspider.pdf.

Appendix C
Spider Websites

American Arachnological Society
www.americanarachnology.org [Google "american arachnology"]
Spider common names; Journal of Arachnology; List of other websites

Jumping Spiders of America North of Mexico
http://spiders.arizona.edu/salticidae/na.salticidae.html
Dr. Wayne Maddison is a jumping spider specialist. Many photographs.

World Spider Catalog
http://research.amnh.org/entomology/spiders/catalog/index.html
American Museum of Natural History site with updated nomenclature and classification of the world's spiders.

Spiders of the Great Smoky Mountains National Park
http://www.dlia.org

Bugguide insect & spider Identification
www.bugguide.net

Appendix D
Photo Credits

Parker Backstrom: 33, 51*br*, 69*t*, 93*t*, 95*m*, 101 *t/b*, 102, 103 *t/bl*, 104, 105 *t/b*, 106, 108, 109 *t/b*, 119 *t/b*, 122 *t/i*, 130, 132, 137*tr*, 178*t*, 179, 186*t*

Giff Beaton [www.giffbeaton.com]: 99*t*, 113*l*, 120, 122*b*, 147, 187*t*, 189*m*

Pete Carmichael [www.awesomespiders.com]: 39*t*, 52, 57, 61*t*, 76, 80, 81, 84, 85*t*, 96, 97*t*, 167*t*, 172, 173, 176, 177, 180*t*, 182, 183*t*, 185 *t/b*, 188, 189 *t/b*, 193 *t/b*, 194, 195*t*

L. L. "Chick" Gaddy: cover *t/br*, title page, *iii*, 1*tr*, 5*b*, 17, 27, 31*br*, 47*b*, 53*t/b*, 55 *t/b*, 56*t*, 58, 61*b*, 71*tl*, 72, 73*bm*, 78, 79, 83 *t/b*, 91*t*, 97*b*, 100 *t/b*, 103*br*, 110, 112, 118, 126, 127, 133*b*, 136*b*, 137 *tl/m*, 163*t*

Marshal Hedin: 23*b*, 30, 31*bl*, 159

Jeff Hollenbeck: 85*b*, 149, 180*b*

Jason Jones: 23*t*

t=top	r=right
m=middle	l= left
b=bottom	i=inset

David Liebman: 36, 37*t*, 41, 43, 56*b*, 77*t*, 82, 97*i*, 113*r*, 133*t*, 154, 184

Tom Murray [www.pbase.com/tmurray74]: 45, 91*b*, 99*b*, 123, 143, 145, 148, 151, 153, 155, 186*b*, 187*b*, 190, 195*b*

Bryan Reynolds [www.bryanreynoldsphoto.com]: 25*t*, 39*b*, 47*t*, 54, 165, 178*b*, 191 *t/b*, back cover spider

Sparky Stensaas [www.sparkyphotos.com]: cover *bl/bm*, 1 *tl/br/bl*, 2, 3, 5*t*, 6*t*, 7 *m/b*, 8 *t/b*, 9, 11*b*, 13*t*, 16, 18, 50, 51 *t/bl*, 59*t*, 62, 63 *t/br/bl*, 64, 65 *t/b*, 68, 69*br*, 70, 71 *tr/ml/b*, 73 *br/bl*, 86, 87 *tl/m/b*, 88, 89*b*, 92, 93 *br/bl*, 94, 95 *t/b*, 98 *t/b*, 105*m*, 107, 111, 116, 117, 121, 128, 129 *t/br/bml/bl*, 136*t*, 137*b*, 140, 141 *t/b*, 158*tl/b*, 162, 163*b*, 164, 166, 167*b*, 170, 171 *t/br/bl*, 174, 175 *t/b*, 181 *t/b*, 183*b*, 192

Larry Weber: 6*b*, 7*t*, 10, 11*t*, 12 *t/m/b*, 13*b*, 14 *t/ml/b*, 15, 25*b*, 31*t*, 37*b*, 59*b*, 77 *i/b*, 89*t*, 90, 131, 135 *t/b*, 150

Index